Song of Songs

The Bible's Great Love Poems in Calligraphy

Margaret Shepherd

mount
tabor
BOOKS

PARACLETE PRESS

BREWSTER, MASSACHUSETTS
BARGA, ITALY

2021 First Printing

Song of Songs: The Bible's Great Love Poems in Calligraphy

Copyright © 2021 by Margaret Shepherd

ISBN 978-1-64060-173-4

The Mount Tabor Books name and logo (mountain with rays of light)
are trademarks of Paraclete Press, Inc.

Library of Congress Cataloging-in-Publication Data
Names: Shepherd, Margaret, illustrator, writer of added commentary.
Title: Song of songs / Margaret Shepherd.
Other titles: Bible. Song of Solomon. English.
Description: Brewster, Massachusetts : Paraclete Press, [2020] | Includes
    bibliographical references. | Summary: "The biblical book, richly
    illustrated in calligraphy, with commentary"— Provided by publisher.
Identifiers: LCCN 2019056967 | ISBN 9781640601734 (hardcover)
Subjects: LCSH: Calligraphy.
Classification: LCC BS1483 .S44 2020 | DDC 223/.9077—dc23
LC record available at https://lccn.loc.gov/2019056967

10 9 8 7 6 5 4 3 2 1

Published by Paraclete Press
Brewster, Massachusetts and Barga, Italy
www.paracletepress.com

Manufactured by Regent Publishing Services Ltd., Hong Kong
Printed August 2021 in Shenzhen, Guangdong, China

Contents

Introduction

ABOUT SONG OF SONGS

Song of Songs, the celebrated biblical book, is made of poems about earthly love. Its main characters are two lovers who speak passionately to each other or rhapsodize about each other: a very young woman and a young man of her town, probably a shepherd. We hear occasionally from a chorus of her female friends, and briefly from her brothers. She is specifically spoken to once as the Shulamite; she sometimes calls him "my king." Scholars can't agree on whether there is also a narrator who comments now and then.

The original language of Song of Songs suggests that it was first composed to be recited aloud 800–600 BCE and was gradually written down over the next few centuries. With very little firm evidence to go on, scholarly opinions differ widely about these dates. Song of Songs was approved for inclusion in the Jewish canon around 100 CE and in the Christian Bible some three centuries later.

Song of Songs does not have a story line, but it pulls together a cluster of forms and topics that focus on the joys of physical love. Its musical equivalent would be a book of Chopin etudes or a song cycle of German lieder, where a variety of short compositions explore different aspects of a common idea. It also compares to other multifaceted works of art such as "The Rubáiyát of Omar Khayyám," in seventy-five quatrains; "Thirteen Ways of Looking at a Blackbird," a poem by Wallace Stevens; or the twenty-five paintings by Claude Monet known as "Haystacks."

Song of Songs is unlike almost every other book of the Bible, in half a dozen ways:

❖ It includes no family trees, no battles, no dietary rules, no legends, no historical events, no religious doctrines, and no promises from God.

❖ Song of Songs does not mention the name of God, and it refers to Solomon in only three places. When Song of Songs does mention Solomon, it is to describe his possessions: his splendid palanquin, his wedding crown, his numberless wives, and his well-managed vineyard. He plays no role and speaks no words.

❖ The young woman's voice and her point of view dominate the scenes and events, an unusual perspective for an era when women had very little social or legal power. She describes her desires in striking detail, boldly pursues her lover, meets him for private trysts, and seizes the initiative in physical love. When she is hurt or disappointed, she pushes back. Her lover, in contrast, does not talk about how he feels, but mainly describes how beautiful she is. In one place, he tries to coax her to come home from the wilderness.

❖ Although Song of Songs comes from a patriarchal society, it makes seven references to mothers but none to fathers. The young woman brings her lover not just to her family home, calling it "my mother's house," but also "into the chamber of her that conceived me." And the crown that King Solomon wears is placed on his head by his mother.

❖ The young woman and those around her scarcely allude to her traditional role of wife and mother. In the last chapter, she speaks with confidence about someday making a success of marriage and a husband—a role that she intends to shape for herself. In this poem about sexual longing, children are not even mentioned.

❖ The verses describe physical love and emotion in language so explicit that some of it still seems too frank today.

Although Song of Songs is so profoundly different from the rest of the Bible and its subject makes so many believers uncomfortable, it has never been out of the canon since its inclusion some 2,000 years ago. It posed a challenge, of course, for those who did not think that frank descriptions of passionate human love belonged in Christian worship. Over the centuries, they have avoided the obvious subject when they explain what the poetry is *about*: Middle Eastern politics, dream analysis, the triumph of the poor over the rich, primitive fertility cults, or mystical hidden messages. Until recently, many scholars were still trying to limit its interpretation to a metaphor of God's love for his chosen people or Christ's relationship with his church.

Those who embraced the sensuality of Song of Songs eventually prevailed over those who were more comfortable with a metaphor. Eighteenth-century Enlightenment poet J. G. von Herder said that those allegories "defied common sense," and Marvin Pope, a twentieth-century authority on the text, compared them to the onlookers in the folktale who would not admit that the emperor has no clothes.

In the second century CE, Rabbi Akiva wrote, "God forbid! [that it should not belong in the canon] . . . for all the writings are holy, but the Song of Songs is the holiest of the holy." Today, most scholars are ready to agree that human passion is its topic, bringing Song of Songs into the love life of a new generation of readers.

ABOUT SCRIBES AND SCRIPTURE

The word of God and the art of the scribe have always brought out the best in each other. Calligraphy adds extra depth to the page, while Scripture elevates a useful craft into a major art. Jews, Christians, and Muslims have all taken pride in calling themselves the "people of the book." And what a book! Western religions owe much of their visual glory—and their very survival—to the art of calligraphy, which made the word of God legible, permanent, and sublime.

The scribes who copied these holy texts wrote at first with flat-nibbed pens made of reed or quill. Beyond a similar set of materials, they also shared the related letterforms of the Hebrew, Greek, Latin, and Arabic letters. Beginning as a set of symbols for commercial transactions around the Mediterranean, the alphabet matured into a phonetic system of great versatility that preserved the Hebrew Bible, evolved into a propaganda tool for the Roman Empire, and carried the new religion of Christianity throughout the known world. Later, the Qur'an was written down in the kindred forms of the Arabic *alif bet*. (Figures a, b, c, d)

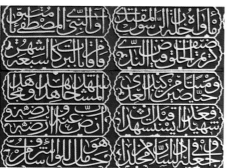

Figures a, b, c, d

Over the centuries, scribes wrote on a succession of surfaces: from papyrus to wax to marble to copper (used for some of the Dead Sea scrolls) to parchment to paper, but always adapting the ABCs to the materials around them. Each generation of calligraphers who copied the Bible found new ways to improve the letters and make them more durable for storage as well as more beautiful to look at. Because the alphabet relied on only some two dozen letter forms, it was, and still is, simpler to learn than any other writing system. Literacy comes easier to societies that write and read with the phonetic ABCs.

The scribe's role, too, evolved over the centuries. Because papyrus scrolls were fragile and needed recopying every few decades, Hebrew scribes strove for accuracy of the text more than decoration of the page. Because parchment, in contrast, lasted for hundreds of years but was costly to produce, Christian scribes compressed the letters to cram each page as full as they could. Until the mid-fifteenth century, such books were produced one at a time as the work of a single scribe or a small team of specialists in painting, rubricating, gold-leafing, and bookbinding. His or her job was to copy God's word exactly and decorate it handsomely. The scriptorium of a monastery or a convent surrounded its calligraphers with rules against interruptions, to prevent errors in copying holy Scripture.

The invention of printing with moveable type—which debuted in 1455 with the magnificent Gutenberg Bible (Figure e) and spread swiftly—transformed the job of Christian scribes, freeing them not only from the toil of copying by hand but also from the dread of making and perpetuating a mistake. Now, once a Bible page was typeset and approved, it could be reproduced hundreds of times without errors creeping in, allowing a definitive edition to be printed, distributed, and studied in virtually identical form, anywhere in the world. The first authorized English translation of the complete Bible printed in England, the majestic 1611 King James Version, was set in a mix of Gothic and Roman type, ornamental

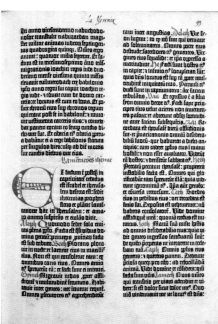

Figure e

capitals, and decorative borders (Figure f). It strongly echoed, in black and white, typography's deep roots in the bygone glory of the handwritten page.

The first type fonts were modeled on the best handwritten Gothic, Roman, and Italic alphabets, and for the next two centuries the work of skilled calligraphers continued to provide the letter models for printing done with type, copperplate, etching, and lithography. But simply copying copies of copies of old letterforms eventually froze them into lifeless formulas, which Charles Rennie MacIntosh decried as "icy perfections," drawn mechanically rather than shaped with hand and eye.

Figure f

During this period of decline, a page of Scripture and images might range from the imitative, cautiously conventional medievalism of Owen Jones (Figure g) to the wildly original, intensely personal mysticism of William Blake (Figure h).

Figures g, h

Figure i

Figure j

Whether they obeyed the rules of traditional calligraphy or resisted them, letter artists were searching for new directions. It took the late-nineteenth-century Arts and Crafts Movement to re-animate letters with the beauty of humanistic calligraphy, when William Morris reintroduced and advocated high standards of handcraftsmanship. His anti-industrial, Utopian visions about better ways to live and work disrupted all the arts and reconnected type design with its roots in calligraphy. Some calligraphers looked to the past for the kind of standards shown in this 1896 Kelmscott Press *Laudes Beatae Mariae Virginis* (Figure i). Some looked to the future. Edward Johnston, an influential teacher, created classic typefaces that would shape graphic design for the next fifty years, from his much-admired traditional capitals for the Doves Press Bible of 1904 (Figure j) to the ultra-modern alphabet for the London Underground.

A subsequent calligraphy revival in the 1970s created a new army of devoted letter artists—many of them first inspired by lessons from Johnston's classic textbook. Some worked to improve the quality of photo-type and digital letters. Some popularized and taught the historic scripts as a hobby. And still others found ways to revive the time-honored connection between scribes and Scripture.

Producing a modern Bible by hand, just as in the Middle Ages, still requires a team. In 1990, polymath Don Knuth enlisted fifty-nine calligraphers to render a single verse, 3:16, from fifty-nine different books of the Bible, to showcase the broad diversity of modern lettering (Figure k). Illustrator Barry Moser teamed up with type designer Matthew Carter in the late 1990s to create the Pennyroyal Caxton Bible, enlisting letter carver John Benson to provide the rubric GOD, CHRIST,

Figure k

and AMEN for its beginning, middle and end (Figure l). In 1998 Donald Jackson initiated design work for *The Saint John's Bible* (Figure m), focusing the talents of artists, biblical scholars, and medievalists on a project that would span more than a decade, combining fourteenth-century materials with twenty-first-century design.

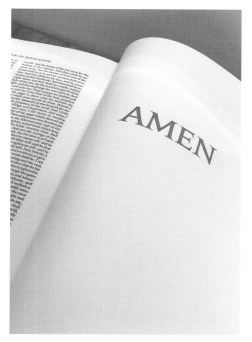

Figure l

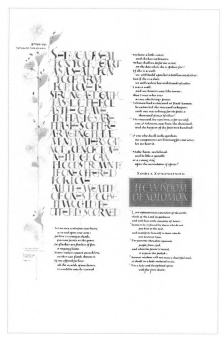

Figure m

Because Song of Songs is read aloud in synagogues during Passover, it has been part of many artists' Haggadah re-designs. Some verses from Song of Songs are also frequent choices for Jewish marriage documents like this dual-language *ketubah* (Sivia Katz, Figure n). Such signed contracts are also an official part of Quaker weddings and an embellishment for many others.

Figure n

Today, despite the allure of high-tech substitutes, people still ask scribes to handwrite the words that really matter: they design memorial plaques, inscribe awards and gifts, coordinate with architects and interior designers, add names to Book of Remembrance pages, design hand-carved gravestones, commemorate church events, and enhance weddings with unique invitations, hand-addressed envelopes, monogrammed keepsakes, and legacies like the traditional *ketubah*. Scripture is a popular choice for both client commissions and artistic designs.

Twenty-first-century calligraphers have the best of both worlds: the continuity of an ancient craft that connects them to their roots plus the stimulus of a modern art that challenges them to innovate. Writing by hand is still a living art just as vibrant, and just as relevant to religion, as the other arts of sculpture, music, architecture, and painting. It gives calligraphers at all levels the pleasure of making beautiful and useful things that connect them to other people. Five hundred years ago, in "In Laude Scriptorium," Johannes Trithemius declared that "The dedicated scribe . . . will never fail to praise God, give pleasure to angels, strengthen the just, convert the sinners, commend the humble, confirm the good, confound the proud and rebuke the stubborn." Calligraphers today still enjoy these blessings.

But it doesn't stop there. Calligraphy offers its devotees something more profound than just feeling happy to be useful. Beyond the beauty they create, the human connections they form, and the benefit they give to others, they are also discovering how much the handwritten word does for their own inner life. Carefully copying a text with pen and ink puts them in touch with *themselves*. As communication gets more impersonal and life gets more materialistic, people seek out calligraphy because it can make the very act of writing feel like a sacrament.

The spiritual benefit of writing by hand was held dear by Abbot Trithemius, who went on to describe it as the scriptorium's ultimate blessing: "While [the scribe] sits in silence and solitude and immerses himself pleasantly in his manuscripts . . . his mind is illumined and his sentiments are enkindled."

Calligraphy and Scripture are good for each other, but they are also good for *you*.

MY LIFE IN CALLIGRAPHY

I have been a calligrapher all my working life, and I have written many beautiful, sacred, and useful items, from name tags and wedding invitations to diplomas and memorial plaques, plus many creative works of art for my own pleasure. I also hand-lettered and illustrated twelve of my books about how to learn and appreciate calligraphy. In my thirties and forties, I experimented off and on with designs for some verses from Song of Songs, returning to it recently to spend five years writing out the complete book. Mindful of the affinity between calligraphy and Scripture, I knew that my own art could help me learn about this text and give me insights to share with others.

I was guided throughout my career by the ideas of other artists. One was type designer Beatrice Warde, who wrote in 1932 that letter style should be like "a crystal goblet," presenting the text without drawing attention to itself. Whenever I chose the letter style, color, scale, and layout, I aimed to help the reader focus on the meaning behind the words, not on the letters themselves. Calligraphy was always a window for me to gain insight into a text, which I trusted would tell me how it wanted me to arrange and letter it.

I also agreed with nineteenth-century sculptor Medardo Rossi, "What I strive most to achieve in art is to make you forget the material." Readers should not be distracted by the physical page; like the audience at a play, they should be able to trust the artist to create a world. They should be getting carried away by the drama, not be critiquing the sets and lighting and stage makeup and period costumes. I found that using precious historical materials made me reluctant to try new designs and experiment with new techniques. By conscious decision, these Song of Songs designs do not rely on medieval pigments, gold leaf, parchment, and quill pens; I prefer the acrylic inks, bond paper, and metal pens of my own era.

I was not born with any special talent for writing the letters that I love; in fact I flunked the transition to the Palmer Method when I was taught cursive in third grade. Later, when I studied the formal Roman alphabet, the professor and I had to spend more than a month on the two strokes that make capital "O." Forming the letters properly was always a struggle for me. My fingers developed calluses; my eyes dried up; sometimes just sitting still made my whole body ache. But the letters always rewarded my work; I felt special gratitude when I succeeded, and I gained special insight into the mind of the beginner when I did not.

Most of all, every day that I pick up the pen, I can count on the threefold pleasure of mastering my craft, being useful, and getting in touch with myself. Like the scribes in Abbot Trithemius's fifteenth-century abbey, my mind is illumined and my sentiments are enkindled. Ink warms the soul.

Song of Songs in Calligraphy

WITH COMMENTARY BY THE ARTIST

I: 1

The very first page establishes the colors and moods of the 44 calligraphy designs that will follow. The poems that form Song of Songs are unified by the poet's voice as it explores many different aspects of earthly love. I intended the first page to illustrate that a medley can add up to unity.

The seven vertical banners are a metaphor for several kinds of diversity: an anthology of poems, a spectrum of views on love and lovers, at least four different voices, a cluster of interpretations. Even the upright staff of the letter "f" is made of many separate strokes. The penstroke banners are each imperfect in a different way; their faded colors and tattered ends bear witness to years of floating in the breeze.

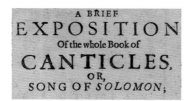

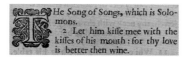

Figure I:1 a, b, c, d

The title is the first chapter's first verse, which has been translated differently over the centuries. For example, Puritan preacher John Cotton, in his 1642 commentaries, worded it four ways in the space of two pages (Figures I:1a, b, c, and d): "The Canticles;" "Song of Songs;" "The Song of Songs, which is Solomon's;" "The Song of Songs."

Scholars also argue about what the title actually means. The phrase Song of Songs may be similar to "crème de la crème," the top of any category. Even the word *is*, in the subtitle, is not from Hebrew but was added by the King James translators. "Is" has been interpreted different ways over the centuries, to mean that Song of Songs is *about* Solomon, *by* Solomon, *dedicated to* Solomon, or *in the style of* Solomon. Other translations update it for their own era: "An Excellent Song Which Was Solomon's" (The Geneva Bible, 1599); "Solomon's finest Song" (The Holman Christian Standard Bible, 1998); "The most beautiful song of Solomon," (The Names of God, 2011); "The Song—best of all songs—Solomon's song!" (The Message, 1993–2002).

Common usage today is "The Song of Solomon" or "Song of Songs."

Song of Songs

Which is Solomon's

Calligraphy by Margaret Shepherd ○ Based on diverse translations

I: 2–4

I have always believed that a letter can be *anything*. But some letters get the spotlight much more often than others. Since capital "Q" is so rare in English scripture, and even capital "O" is relatively uncommon, I was happy that the text of Song of Songs was filled with the calligraphic luxury known as the "vocative O," literally an "O" that calls to you. Its visual form accommodates a hundred different visual ideas.

Some of the emotions in Song of Songs are so intense that they can only be expressed by speaking directly to the beloved, saying "O my soul," and "O, my dove," or occasionally addressing the chorus, "O daughters of Jerusalem." In Latin, this is expressed in the vocative case by changing a few letters at the end of the noun. In English, such a sentence starts with "O." Until a generation ago, English translators used this formal "O" to show that the poet is not speaking *about* someone but *to* someone.

I have felt special affection for the letter "O" ever since I encountered Alastair Reid's charming poem "The O-Filler," about a man whose life quest, it seems, is to fill in every "o" in his local library. As a beginning calligrapher, I practiced capital "O" for a whole month until its center was a perfect oval. In Song of Songs, I found myself preferring translations that included "O" because often it could help the design make more sense of the text. A dozen of my designs feature the vocative "O" or an O-word such as "Our" and "Over." In the first chapter, for instance, capital "O" plays the role of a burning torch, a eucalyptus wreath, and a golden braid. In later chapters, "O" is a knothole, a signet seal, and, in the very last verse, a setting sun.

Note that a vocative "O" is different from "oh." That word is a modern, offhand interjection; it is not addressed to anyone but just thrown into a written sentence to mimic the cadence of spoken words, as in, "Oh! What a surprise!" To illustrate, compare "Oh God," which starts a complaint, with "O God," which starts a prayer.

YOUR LOVE IS SWEETER THAN WINE TO ME;

Let us make haste;

draw me in your footsteps;

and bring me, O my king into your chambers;

your love will be our joy and our gladness;

your caresses are more precious to me

FRAGRANT IS THE SCENT OF YOUR FRANKINCENSE;

your name is as a perfume poured out;

THEREFORE ALL THE PEOPLE LOVE YOU!

than the finest wine.

How right it is to love you!

O MY BELOVED,

that you would kiss me with
the kisses of your mouth!

SONG *of* SONGS

Which is Solomon's I: 2~4

I: 5–6

These verses used to stop readers in their tracks, put off by that single poorly translated word, "but." The Hebrew is ambiguous, however, meaning either "but" or "and." The translators of the King James Version chose the apologetic construction, "I am black, but comely," because sunburnt skin was a sign of low status and outdoor labor, an age-old stigma that began to change only two generations ago. Recent translations improve the tone with "I am weathered but still elegant" (The Message 1993–2004) or "I am black and beautiful" (Revised Standard Version 1946).

The young woman still wants to explain how her skin got so dark. She has been forced by her brothers to do field work, but she turns it into a badge of honor. A few scholars think it might also be that dark skin makes her different from the other girls, more robust and athletic. I enlarged the words that celebrate her darkness. These lines of lettering suggest the outlines of a torso, with the upright body language of pride and confidence. Her legs are planted firmly and her shoulders are thrown back. She is boyish but also beginning to have curves. She may be the same "little sister" that the brothers are so worried about in VIII: 8–9; but even while they try to dominate her, she is proud of who she is.

The plaid banner that surrounds her repeats the fourth line, where she compares herself to the richest of tapestries. I built it up out of purple shades to look like the soft mauve that many dyes used to fade away into, with the slubs and mis-weaves of handwoven fabrics. I rounded it to seem like a sash or loosened belt that protects her while it restrains her.

These verses introduce vineyard imagery that will recur throughout Song of Songs. Vineyards are owned, rented out, supervised, and mismanaged; vineyards demand hard labor; vineyards are public but also private; vineyards are vulnerable to vandalism. Lovers make love in the shade of vineyards, and everyone drinks wine made from their grapes. This young woman is rightly proud of her time laboring there.

O ye daughters of Jerusalem,
I AM DARK, AND
I AM BEAUTIFUL.
Dark like the tents of Kedar;
Lavish as Solomon's tapestries;
Do not stare at how much
the sun has scorched me;
For my brothers were angry
with me; they made me keep
their vineyards; yet mine
own vineyard
have I not
kept.

Chapter I:
SONG of SONGS

verses 5-6
which is Solomon's

I: 7–8

Although it is thousands of years since our alphabet letters have looked like the pictures they came from—ever since the Greeks simplified an Egyptian drawing of an ox head to stand for the sound of *aleph*—letters seem to still be trying to revive the golden age when they were drawings of creatures.

I have always thought that letters were alive and only waiting to be noticed. As a young child, I was sure that every bar of piano music in my beginner's lesson book had a flock of lambs across the bottom; only later did I learn that they were a nineteenth-century copyist's abbreviation for the word "Pedal." (Figure I: 7-8, a)

Figures I: 7-8 a and b

Calligraphic sheep showed up in my life again when I came across a Celtic letter "W" that seemed to personify a sheep for the word "wool." (Figure I: 7-8 b) I could not resist helping the W's in the main paragraph of this design look like little sheep resting in grass. I even found one at the end of the final word "meadow." The string of green squares under each w could suggest uneven meadow grass, or distant hills. Other letters reinforced invisible qualities. I used Ronde lettering, with its roundest alternate letters, to support the image of cool shade, resting sheep, and soft wool.

Although I loved helping those Ws turn back into sheep, the most important task of my design was to accommodate the two distinct voices of the lovers. The young woman asks, "Where are you?" and then frets that following the young man too openly might give her a bad reputation. He answers, "Here's how to find me." It's possible that she may just be remembering or imagining his voice in her head, as an excuse to go looking for him.

I used lines of small, plain Bookhand letters for the first and last verses. They could be quotation marks bracketing the main text, or noonday shadows, or two final clusters of sheep arriving at the meadow with a few stragglers trailing behind. I scattered the words of the citation like hoofprints for the young woman to follow.

Tell me,

my soul's beloved,

where
do your
sheep
lie down
to rest
at noon?

Where do you graze your flock? To find you, I would have to put on a veil and ask every one of your friends to tell me where you have gone with your sheep. To find me, my beloved, simply let the hoofprints of my flock lead you up into the meadow.

There we
will leave
your lambs

to drowse in the shade

of the shepherds'

tents.

SONG of SONGS
Which is Solomon's

I: 9–11

In these verses, the young man compares his beloved to the most beautiful animal he can think of—a precious purebred mare. I had no trouble embracing this metaphor to create the visual images here, because for most of my own adolescence, I too believed that nothing could be more enjoyable than looking at, stroking, riding, drawing, and thinking about horses. It is an infatuation that I understand perfectly.

I have, however, met many women who do not long to be compared to a horse. I especially wanted this design to convince such skeptics of the grace, spirit, timelessness, and cultural resonance that horses embody. Every curve and motion of a horse can find its echo in the body and gestures of a young woman. In my design, the horse's profile evokes the curves of a woman's torso. Horses have flowing manes and tails, with decorations often braided into them; they can be draped with richly decorated blankets, tassels, and streamers; their tack is often ornamented with jewels. For those who live with them, they are objects of care and attention. Ever since humans tamed them, horses have required diligent attention and careful grooming. A few translators of this verse think it can also refer to how even the most docile mare can drive stallions crazy.

Calligraphers know that every choice of letter style, size, and spacing changes the tone of voice and creates an atmosphere. I chose earthy colors to evoke the world of stables, leather, hair, and hooves. Celtic lettering is solid and organic, conveying gravity without formality, strength without bulk. Italic lettering echoes the supple motion of the mare's mane and tail. Without wanting to overwork the metaphor, I lined up green and aqua shapes to look like round turquoises and square emeralds, the "rows of jewels" that are draped over the woman's body or lined up on the mare's bridle cheekpieces.

In one small detail, I added more Celtic decoration by filling the capital "O" with intricate yellow and purple interlacing. This can suggest the braided hair of either a woman or a mare, as well as the intertwined ribbons of gold and silver jewelry mentioned in the text.

I have likened thee,
my beloved,
to a young mare
of pharaoh's chariot,

For thy cheeks
are lovely between
rows of jewels,
thy neck is wreathed
with chains of gold.
We will braid for thee
ribbons of finest gold
studded with silver.

SONG of SONGS I:9~11
which is Solomon's

I: 12–14

Sometimes the words practically take charge and design the page themselves. In the verses here, the initials "W" and "M" of "While the King" and "My Beloved" form mirror images of each other. Beginning calligraphers are taught to look for congruent pairs of letters that look like each other when rotated 180 degrees (Figure I: 12-14, a), such as Roman V and A; Bookhand u and n; Italic *b* and *q*. Virtually every alphabet style has some of these

V A u n b q

Figure I:12-14 a

pairs; it is what makes the letters work as a harmonious team instead of having to be read one at a time as unique individuals. And, as with so many letters, I needed to add only a few clues to transform them into living creatures. I made the upper letter, W, large, colorful, and framed by stiff wing feathers, and made the lower letter, M, small, drab, and trailed by softer wings. This reflects nature's frequent contrast between male and female birds. I gave her one bright tail feather that echoes a corresponding empty space in the upper bird. Also, for those familiar with Hebrew calligraphy, the upper bird's feathers evoke Hebrew serifs. (Figure I: 12-14, b)

Not only do the W and M balance each other visually— they are clearly a couple—but their beaks touch like two birds meeting in a midair rendezvous. I also arranged the citation to suggest a small sprig of myrrh held between them in their beaks, since it is mentioned in the text as "lying between my breasts."

Figure I:12-14 b

A few Song of Songs verses use metaphors that rely on Old Testament place names. Each time I encountered them, I researched them to see if they helped throw any light on the text. Known over thousands of years for their size and fertility, "the vineyards of Engedi" are now an Israeli national park that lies along the western shore of the Dead Sea. The poet's original audience would have recognized its significance, but to bring this allusion to life for today's readers, I used a translation that added the evocative words "oasis" and "far-off."

HILE THE KING
sits at his banquet,
my lavender breathes
forth its soft fragrance.
A bouquet of myrrh is my
well~beloved unto me,
that shall lie all night
betwixt my breasts.

Y BELOVED
is to me as a cluster
of henna blossoms
in the vineyards
by the oasis of
far~off Engedi.

SONG of SONGS
Which is Solomon's
I: 12~14

I: 15

This verse challenged me to make softness visible with pen and ink. I wanted the words themselves to look as light as a feather. This called for soft letters, narrow pens, and generous spacing. My choice was a blend of Ronde script capitals, with a Celtic lowercase "d" added in. The curved ascender of that final d looked like a dove to me. I used it again in II: 14, in the line "O my dove." (Figure I: 15) I took the opportunity here to follow the loops and overlaps of a feathery swash, shaping it into a downy nest below the simple Bookhand text.

Figure I:15

The words of the King James Version translation made sense until I looked at them a little more carefully. Although the poet clearly refers to something soft, shy, and fluttering, doves actually have small, beady, black, expressionless eyes. It's their bodies and feathers—and the whispery cooing sounds they make—that are as soft as a young woman's glance seen behind her feathery eyelashes. While the King James translates this as "thou hast doves' eyes," the Revised Standard Version makes a more general comparison that "your eyes are doves," which may be more faithful by allowing more room for interpretation. The dove metaphor adds an extra layer of meaning, because doves mate for life and stay faithful to each other.

I arranged my pair of nesting doves to form the initial "B." While mixing some soft gray ink, however, I had to stop and answer a deceptively simple question: What color *is* a dove? Of course, white doves would look purest and sweetest, but I needed them to show up on a background of white paper. I searched dozens of photographs for a dove-inspired tint from the spectrum of pearly gray, blush pink, pale copper, silver, beige, and mauve. (Figure I: 15, b) I even took time to check out the colors of our local pigeon population, since they are just doves with a less glamorous name. I ended up making the letter silver-gray and partly filling it with a graded wash of warm coral pink.

ƐHOLD,
you are
beautiful,
my beloved, so
very beautiful.
Your eyes are
soft, like doves.

I: 15

Which is Solomon's

SONG of SONGS

I: 16–17

Sometimes the stately tone of the King James Version puts a lid on the passion of the poetry. When the lover says "Behold, thou art fair, my beloved, yea, pleasant," I felt compelled to go looking for warmer words. Because scholars disagree about who is speaking, I chose a version with "handsome," a gender-neutral adjective that lets the lovers admire each other equally, and I added the speaker's "happy" feelings of pleasure in lieu of more lines about physical beauty.

I arranged that first verse in a halo, like yellow sunshine backlighting the wreath of branches. Although the lovers may be sleeping outside, a common scenario in Song of Songs, they describe the trees and branches around them as the beams and rafters of their house. To evoke the sun slanting into the lower corner of this imaginary room, I wrote the citation in the same yellow that shines in from overhead. I was inspired by remembering "lovers alone wear sunlight," a line from E. E. Cummings, a minister's son who was steeped in the language of Scripture.

The main text describes the lovers' delight in watching the sunlight fall through the green branches above them. "Green" covers a wide range of colors, as visual artists discover when they learn to look objectively. I was happy to find that the spectrum of green leaves extended to include my favorite verdigris, ecru, lavender, chartreuse, khaki, and slate blue. These are all color names that I loved learning to pronounce as a girl.

The design needed the letters of the main verse to be large—and flawless. Because Bookhand is my favorite letter style, I always welcome the chance to render its lovely proportions, intuitive spacing, subtle family resemblances, and graceful thicks and thins. Readers today, however, are so used to pixel-perfect Roman lower-case type that there is no room for human error in its hand-lettered counterpart. If the lettering and spacing stray even slightly out of proportion, readers may not be able to pinpoint the problem, but it will still distract them from Bookhand's visual pleasure. Accordingly, I rehearsed these seven words for hours, until I felt sure that the text was letter-perfect but would still evoke a human voice.

O beloved, how handsome you are; you make me so happy!

OUR BED is shaded with green branches;

The beams of our house are cedar trees, and our rafters are of cypress.

SONG *of* SONGS
Which is Solomon's

I: 16 ~ 17

II: 1–2

I grew up reading the Bible in a 1948 Revised Standard Version (Figure II: 1-2, a and b), absorbing its page layout along with its lessons. Each book began with one moderately ornate black and white initial. Although it was simple, I know now that I was lucky my Bible offered *any* decoration at all; the King James Version of my era had only the smallest, barest capitals. (Figure II: 1-2, c and d) No wonder a new generation of calligraphers welcomed the chance to revive the decorated pages of the past!

Figures II:1-2 a, b

Like most beginning calligraphers, I was content to imitate the medieval and Renaissance tradition of embellishing the first letter of the first word of Scripture, poetry, or prose, and placing it in the page's upper left corner. The Western alphabet is

Figures II:1-2 c, d

the world's only writing system that offers two separate letterforms, giving letter artists of the Western world an extra tool to shape the page. Unfortunately, many calligraphers don't move past the standard template shown here (Figure II: 1-2, e), to explore new ways to design with capitals.

Figure II:1-2 e

While I enjoyed learning from centuries-old designs (and still do), I found myself hungry for more freedom of choice about *which* initial to enlarge, since sentences in English are most likely to start with the uninspiring "I" and "T." When I began *Song of Songs*, I sensed that many of its verses held crucial words that I should emphasize, often words from the middle of a sentence or a paragraph, words with an uncommon first letter that would sustain a fresh metaphor and offer the viewer a new experience.

When I began to sketch designs for "I am the Rose of Sharon," I saw that the standard choice of initial, "I," could offer nothing like the visual complexity of the capital "R," which could suggest the leaf, stem, and flower of the lily. Additionally, I'm convinced that letters have feelings. So simply because "R" doesn't get to start sentences very often, I was happy to let it play a starring role.

I am a ROSE of Sharon, a lily of the valleys, As a lily among the brambles, so is my beloved among the young maidens.

Even while its message stayed the same, the Bible as a book changed over the centuries. New translations helped it keep pace with changes in spoken language, with many corrections to spelling and grammar. Beyond that, however, many of the letters, words, and numbers that we now take for granted as part of the "original" text were added and standardized more recently, mainly for convenience. The chapter divisions, for instance, were the work of thirteenth-century scholars. Verse numbers were added in the sixteenth century; you won't find them, for instance, in hand-copied Bibles such as the Book of Kells. Invoking artistic license as well as historical precedent, I removed those little verse numbers from the text and bundled them with the chapter number to create a line of citation for each cluster of verses I grouped together. In the verse here, which compares the beloved to the shade of an apple tree, the citation helps reinforce one more curved swash of the leafy flourish.

Rethinking where to put chapter and verse did not mean that I treated them as optional, *ever*. I always used the whole line somewhere on the page. I enjoyed finding inventive ways to integrate it into the page as an organic part of the Scripture, factoring it into the design from the very first pencil thumbnail sketches.

The citations throughout Song of Songs range from tiny and meek to bold and conspicuous. Four representative examples are shown below. (Figures II: 3, a, b, c, d)

a. This citation forms a small line at the outer edge of a large whirling galaxy. V: 2–7.

b. Divided in four parts, this citation is used to establish the corners of the design. VII: 6–10.

c. This citation runs vertically, separating the narrator from the memory of her trauma. V: 7–8.

d. Written in over-sized, almost abstract Gothic, this citation fences in a formal garden. VI: 1–3

SONG of SONGS II: 3

Which is Solomon's

As the apple tree
among the trees of the
wood, *so is my beloved*
among the young men.
I sit in his shadow
with delight, and
his fruit is sweet
to my taste.

I'm partial to purple for calligraphy. Purple carries a lot of weight. It has long symbolized everything rich, rare, and royal: it used to be extremely expensive. It was a "fugitive" color that faded in sunlight. It doesn't get drowned out by other strong colors such as scarlet or brown, and it can be almost as intense as black while still adding color to the page. Purple makes other colors look good, both the blues and greens near it on the color wheel and the complementary yellows and oranges on the other side.

All through *Song of Songs*, I've used purple ink in places where many calligraphers might have automatically written in black. In fact, black does not let any light reflect off its surface. Because what appears black in nature is made of many colors, artists learn to look carefully at the real colors and interpret them faithfully. Oil painters, watercolorists, and weavers are taught to be leery of black, and of letting it mix with other pigments or dyes. Calligraphers find that India ink may corrode a metal pen, and it will often ruin a watercolor brush. Rather than default to the standard black ink of historical calligraphy and typography, I have let each text suggest what color I might use to strengthen the meaning.

The purple in this design suggests ripe grapes. While "his banquet house" could refer to a large and formal building, many translators acknowledge that it may mean a much humbler shelter in the vineyards where a courting couple could meet for a tryst. I chose Celtic capitals, a practical, more informal style than Roman ones, to help the viewer imagine a small, intimate spot. The purple lettering across the top alludes to the banner mentioned in the texts. It complements the rainbow of braided and twisted cords, which suggest a curtain screening the entrance, creating a private space. The interlaced knots at the top of each cord echo the Celtic motif.

The small letters that describe intimate details of the lovers embracing are gathered into a soft, protected, organic shape. I wrote them in purple letters, too, using the simplest Bookhand to avoid distracting from the intensity of the words.

He Led me to his Banquet house,
and his Banner over me was Love.

Let me
lie among blossoms;
comfort me with apples,
for I am faint with desire.
I feel his left hand beneath
my head, while his right
hand holds me close.

II: 7

In this verse the young woman speaks to her friends, the "daughters of Jerusalem," entreating them to be cautious about love. It will grow and mature, but only if the lovers use caution and do not rush it. I chose the growing plant (Figure II: 7) as my own visual metaphor for the love described in these verses.

This warning carries special weight, because unlike any other verse in *Song of Songs*, it is repeated almost verbatim three times (above). It brackets the book, appearing for the first time here, next in III: 5, and once near the end.

Figure II:7

Although the lines appear to spiral around the center, they can in fact be read in conventional order from left to right and top to bottom. This design shows the words coiled inside a small seed or bulb, which seems to be dormant but is actually so eager to sprout that a small leaf at its center has already started to unfurl and the "f" in "before" has begun to grow.

Translators have rendered this verse in the King James Version as, "I charge you . . . that ye stir not up, nor awake my love, till he please," and in the Revised Standard as, "I adjure you . . . that you stir not up nor awaken love until it please." Though they both make sense, I preferred other translations that warn not to arouse love "before it is ready," or "before its time," so as to create the image of slow growth, not a slumbering man.

I have translated the name of the chorus as "Daughters of Zion" elsewhere, but here I needed the extra length of the virtually synonymous "Daughters of Jerusalem" to help form a leaf. In addition, after checking many dictionaries, I felt strongly that "wild deer and gazelles" would be more familiar to the modern reader than the "roes and hinds" of four centuries ago.

SONG OF SONGS, Which is Solomon's O ye daughters of Jerusalem, I caution you, by the wild deer and gazelles of the field, stir not up nor arouse love, before it has ripened. Chapter II: Verse 1

II: 8–9

These two verses left me deeply puzzled. This young girl is being spied on; how does she feel about that? How *can* she feel?! It is hard for a modern female reader not to cringe because that's how she herself would react. I searched for translations and commentary that could help me make sense out of this passage, to offer some deeper meaning than the forbidden thrill of peering into a window at night.

The young woman inside the window knows that her lover is spying on her. She describes him standing at her window. She says that she feels his gaze. While a modern woman might find this creepy, this young woman—or the poet imagining her—seems to enjoy it. The verses make it clear that she is a willing participant in this seduction, not a victim or a passive object. She owns the experience. She takes pleasure in being looked at, and she actually feels good about the pleasure he gets from looking at her. It's a complex, almost counterintuitive idea, and I had to understand it myself before I tried to portray it.

The strange and haunting image of the young man lingering like an inquisitive gazelle outside her window sets the scene. To focus attention on these words, first I wrote them in an intense blue Bookhand, placed like three crossbars across the shutter, encouraging viewers to read them first. Curiosity will then eventually lead them to decipher the letters in the background.

The layout creates the illusion of looking into a lighted room from outside in the dark. I wrote the first verse vertically in large letters and filled the spaces around them with abstract lines to suggest weathered wood grain. There were enough O's scattered through this text to treat them like stylized knotholes. I filled their centers with soft yellow to imitate light shining behind a shutter, and I added small yellow squares, triangles, strokes, and circles that glow between the uneven planks like cryptic runes.

With the design nearly complete, I chose one circle and filled it with bright green, to give the viewer the kind of jolt that comes from suddenly connecting with someone in the dark.

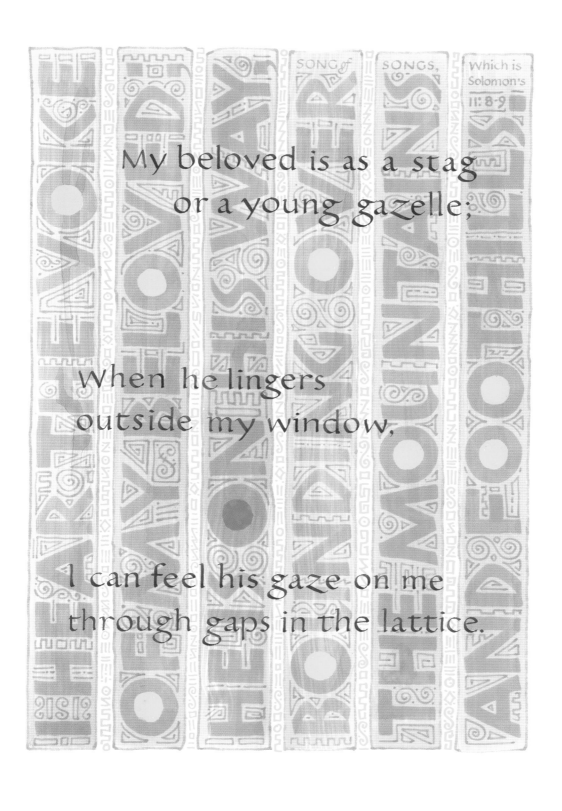

SONG of SONGS, Which is Solomon's 11: 8-9

My beloved is as a stag
or a young gazelle;

When he lingers
outside my window,

I can feel his gaze on me
through gaps in the lattice.

II: 10–13

This is one of the most beloved passages in Song of Songs, a favorite text for marriage ceremonies, wedding gifts, and anniversary celebrations. While its King James Version translation needed very few edits, it did benefit from two. First, what we now call a "turtle dove" was known in 1611 by its nickname "turtle;" I did not want to perpetuate this confusion. Second, the first three words started with the archaic phrase "My beloved spake," a verb form that was already old-fashioned in its time and obsolete soon after. Though it is charming, and the reader can figure it out, it distracts from the timelessness of the text. Most versions update it to "spoke."

Because readers are so familiar with this translation, I wanted to keep the design simple. The lush landscape appeals to sight, sound, and smell, with spring warmth, young figs, fragrant vines, blooming flowers, a chorus of soft bird calls, the voice of a single dove, and the memory of recent rain.

Although it is not featured in the text, or even specifically named, I used a central rose to symbolize this season of new life. It took me a lot of rearranging to position the right letter behind that rose. While the M that begins the first word might seem like the logical place to put a capital, it would pull the visual center too far off balance to the left side and direct attention onto the speaker rather than the beloved. In fact, throughout *Song of Songs*, I looked for ways to shift the emphasis away from "I" and "me" to "beloved" and "you." Sometimes this involved relocating the words, adding color, using different line breaks, or carefully changing the letter size, but whenever I could add visual emphasis by capitalizing a word, I did that too.

Furthermore, this B surrounds the rose with a hint of greenery without becoming too literal. I painted an extra leaf further down the stem, and then constructed one more out of tiny green letters. I painted the capital B with rich dark green, shaped the wet ink with my thumbprint, and then gave it extra texture with a thin tracery of gold scrollwork.

my **B**eloved
spoke,

and said
unto me:

*Arise, my love, my fair
one, and come away.*

For, lo, the winter is past,
the rain is over and gone,
The flowers are blooming,
the season of birdsong has
come, the voice of the turtledove is heard in our land.
Young figs are in bud upon
their verdant branches,
and the blossoming vines
put forth their fragrance.

SONG *of* SONGS
Which is Solomon's
II: 10 ~ 13

Although the meaning of this short verse was clear, each translation offered me a different tone of voice. There are a half dozen English versions that describe a crack in a rock where a young girl—or at least a dove—might hide: "the secret places of the stairs" was too elaborate; "crannies" sounded too playful; "holes" seemed too prosaic. I ended up liking "cleft" and "crevices."

I also kept the antiquated pronouns from the King James Version, feeling that they made the tone of voice gentler and more intimate. "Thy voice" sounded better than "your voice" for coaxing a shy dove.

All through *Song of Songs*, whenever the design process bogged down I simply stopped and read the verses out loud. I am convinced that the words know what they want their design to be; it is each calligrapher's job to discover that goal and help them get there. The beloved here is addressed as a hesitant creature hiding in a crevice. Because the verse divides into two phrases of similar length, I arranged them to form two sides of a cleft rock. I made the separation even clearer by choosing letters of contrasting size, style, and color. To keep the letters neatly packed between straight margins, I shrank the words "in the," "the," and "of the."

Owen Barfield, fellow Inkling and friend of C. S. Lewis, once said, "You cannot make poetry by cunningly removing all the clues." Artists have not done their job if their reader is confused. It is the additional responsibility of every calligrapher to show the reader *where to start reading*, just as an architect designing a building has to show the visitor clearly *where to enter*. To guide the reader, I used large letters in bright blue for the first line, middle-sized letters in slate blue Bookhand for the next phrase, and small letters in gray Italic for the last phrase.

I chose the lily because its flower has always reminded me of a sleeping dove. Its softly furled shape is further echoed here in the shape of the d in dove.

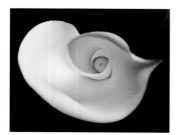

Figure II:14

O my dove,
that art in the cleft
of the rock,
in the secret
crevices
of the cliff.

Let
me see
thy face;
let me hear
thy voice,
for sweet
is thy voice,
and thy face is lovely.

SONG of SONGS II: 14
Which is Solomon's

This design offers an impression of the elusive little creatures that delight to do so much damage. Foxes are notoriously destructive, often creating messy disruption without much gain to themselves, such as killing all the hens in a henhouse while eating only one.

But this is a verse about love, not foxes. It warns those in love to guard against the kind of troublemaker who will try to come between even the most loving couple just to see what happens. I wanted to develop this metaphor, to show how outside meddling can sabotage a relationship. I aimed to make a beautiful design look as though it had been vandalized.

I chose dark green to let the larger letters suggest grapevine overhead. (Using green ink ruled out Celtic lettering, which would have automatically suggested St. Patrick's Day and all things Irish.) I made the capital C out of grapevine trimmings, outlining them with pale yellow as if backlit by sunshine.

The broad triple helix puts the lettering in two twined strands, to signal that the couple may already be in jeopardy because a third strand of evasive, invasive little foxes has already insinuated itself into their midst. At that point, I had to stop and ask myself, what color *is* a fox? I found that fox fur can be red, orange, brown, yellow, gray, or white. I lined up the colors to evoke creatures streaking by, barely glimpsed—now you see them, now you don't.

I have used plain black ink sparingly in my *Song of Songs* designs, even for lettering, but I needed it here to suggest a fox's feet, nose, and ear tips. To balance the letters, I gave the helixes a black background, with an overlay of earth-colored scrollwork in dark burnt umber.

The extra dots along the helix, the widely spaced letters of the citation, the shredded capital C of the title, and the little broken-off branch at the lower corner— this clutter reminds us how easy it is for the mischief of outsiders to cause a world of chaos and hurt.

CATCH THE LITTLE FOXES

Catch them, for those sly little prowling mischief-makers, our grapevines have just begun to blossom and the vineyards; before they spoil bear fruit.

CHAPTER II: VERSE 15

SONG of SONGS

Which is

Solomon's

II: 16–17

Translucent ink and a springy metal pen helped me give these letters what calligraphers call *sparkle*, a subtle and much-admired effect that lets the texture of the paper show through. A little letup of pressure in the middle of the stroke makes the pen nib slightly narrower and the ink slightly less dense.

Like vibrato for violinists and singers, sparkle gives rich depth to a raw pen stroke. It is one of the refinements that has always elevated calligraphy above its counterparts in letterpress, woodblock, silkscreen, or lithography. Even today, digital scanning may capture it but a digital stylus can't create it. Sparkle is also a kind of high-wire act that reveals a scribe's level of skill. It demands a sure, steady stroke and is almost impossible to retouch if the hand falters. Repetitive warmup strokes, using a flexible, broad-edged pen with transparent dye-based ink, will develop control.

The smaller gray Italic lettering between the lines of large blue letters is meant to evoke the oblique light of evening—or maybe morning. Since biblical scholars don't agree about whether the original words in these verses describe dusk or dawn, I simply set the lines of lettering at a shallow angle to suggest the slant of light at either end of the day.

Although I usually prefer not to add a picture to a page where the words have already drawn one, here there was space for a little vignette of a landscape that echoes the words about a gazelle or young deer coming home from the mountains. Like many medieval miniatures, the framed view extends out of the frame.

The ancient names mentioned in Song of Songs don't always help the modern reader visualize a specific place. Some scholars think that "the mountains of Bether" in the King James Version are not meant to be specific mountains but a generic term in Hebrew for mountainous terrain. I chose a translation that described them, with a universal appeal to the senses, as "where fragrant spices grow."

He pastures his flock among the lilies:

my Beloved

As day breathes cool and shadows lengthen,

is mine, and

turn, then, beloved,

I am

II: 16–17

like a gazelle or a young deer

my beloved's

from the mountains where fragrant spices grow.

SONG of SONGS, which is Solomon's

III: 1–4

These four verses tell the story of a young girl's solitary longing, her daring search to find her beloved, her encounter with the night watchmen, and her ultimate success, when she finds the beloved she has ached for and boldly brings him home. It is not a poem about love in general, but a step-by-step drama that unfolds in suspense and leads to a happy ending. I wanted to find a design that would reinforce this dramatic narrative.

I made the language and letter style just formal enough to dignify her desperation, modernizing the archaic verb "loveth," but keeping the proper grammar in "sought" and "whom." I placed this key phrase at the convergence of narrow columns that suggest the labyrinth of streets so typical of a small village. (Figure, III: 1-4, a) I went through many drafts to keep the reader from reading any unintended images into the layout, such as a cross or a flower or a pinwheel.

Figure III:1-4 a

Figures III:1-4 b, c

Inside the gray walls of her house the narrator, symbolized by the vertical pen stroke of the first-person capital letter I (Figure III: 1-4 b), stands at a small lighted window, gazing out at the other houses dotted around her darkened neighborhood. The square can also suggest the bed where she lies alone and sleepless. A careful search shows that another window in the sleeping village is lit up, too (Figure III: 1-4 c), showing that her beloved is out there lying awake and longing for her.

Rather than just arranging horizontal lines of letters in vertical columns, I set almost everything at an angle, to evoke the anxiety and disequilibrium created by her passionate longing. The reader's eye keeps coming back to that central declaration of need. In the midst of their unfulfilled yearning, only these two people are calm and balanced, secure in knowing what they want. For her, the lonely bed in her mother's house is the center of the universe. Its guiding star is her lover's window glowing somewhere nearby.

Night after night, alone on my bed, I sought him whom my soul loves: I sought him, but I found him not: I called him, but he gave no answer.

I SOUGHT HIM WHOM MY HEART LONGS FOR

THE NIGHT WATCHMEN FOUND ME AS THEY MADE THEIR ROUNDS IN THE CITY: I BEGGED THEM, "HAVE YOU SEEN HIM WHOM MY SOUL LOVES?"

Scarcely had I left them, when I found my beloved: I held him and would not let him go, until I had brought him into the house of my mother, into the chamber of her that conceived me.

I SAID, "I WILL RISE NOW AND GO ABOUT THE CITY; THROUGH THE STREETS AND SQUARES I WILL SEEK HIM WHOM MY SOUL LOVES."

III: 1-4
SONG of SONGS
which is Solomon's

III: 5

I n this verse the young woman speaks to her friends, the "daughters of Jerusalem," entreating them to be careful about love. It will grow and mature, but only if the lovers use caution and do not rush it. I chose the growing plant as my own visual metaphor for the love described in these verses.

This warning carries special weight, because, as I noted above in II: 7, unlike any other verse in Song of Songs, it is repeated almost verbatim three times. It brackets the book, appearing twice near the beginning and once near the end.

The second design in this series shows the seedling beginning to grow. A bright green sprout carefully probes the world around it, questing toward the light. I wanted it to look firm but breakable, like the familiar beansprout that combines irresistible growth with delicate fragility. Love is hurt more by growing too fast than by slowing down.

This cautious little plant maintains visual continuity through its ink color, letter style, and organic form as it goes through stages of growth and change. I browsed in greenhouses and pored over seed catalogs before deciding on the colors and shapes of plant growth. Its curves have to be firm and structural, arched but not coiled, to support what the plant is trying to become.

I also went looking for real botanical details to sharpen the resemblance. The green tinge in the middle will be familiar to any cook who has cut open an overripe garlic clove. The small leaf shapes flanking the sprout represent the *cotyledons* that appear on baby plants before the true leaves emerge. And at its base, the descending stroke of the small f in "before" (Figure III: 5) has expanded into a tiny branching rootlet.

Figure III:5

O ye
daughters
of Jerusalem,

I caution
you,

the wild deer and

gazelles of the field,

Stir not up nor arouse love,

SONG OF SONGS, which is Solomon's

III: 5

(By

Before it has ripened.

III: 6–11

These verses urge the daughters of Zion to behold King Solomon's ceremonial procession. He is surrounded by an honor guard, and his crown looms over-head among perfumed "pillars of smoke." This soaring vista is created by generous use of white space, a crucial concept that permeates not only the visual arts, but also music, dance, drama, and literature. As artist Susan Kanaga put it in *The Ecumenism of Beauty*, "What is the presence of absence?"

When students begin calligraphy they usually have to be taught that the white space on the page matters more than the ink. Space is everywhere, shaping everything: inside most letters, between letters, between lines of letters, and all around paragraphs of letters. This principle connects calligraphy to the other two-dimensional arts, where space is also just as important as images and gives the images their power. Japanese painting, for example, relies on virtuoso use of empty space. (Figure III: 6-11) White space is never really empty; it speaks as eloquently as words.

Figure III:6-11

In three dimensions, sculptors define space as the shape of the air inside and around their sculpture. Architects, too, insist that what they design is not primarily the buildings that enclose space, but the spaces themselves, which open over time to create a fourth dimension.

What you hear is even full of empty space. Composers and performers from Wolfgang Mozart to Miles Davis have agreed that music is not only in the notes, but also in the silences between them. The best poetry, prose, and drama contain no extra words because authors know that they can let the reader's imagination do some of the work. Even stand-up comedians know the importance of letting a beat of silence double the punch of their punch lines.

King Solomon is an empty space, conspicuous by his absence. The verses here mainly describe the soldiers who accompany him, the litter that carries him, and the crown he wears—and his mother crowning him. The letters of his name are empty of color. This is one of only three designs that even mention him; in the book named after him, King Solomon himself does not speak.

Who is this that cometh out of the wilderness like pillars of smoke, with the perfume of frankincense and myrrh, with all exquisite spices? Behold Solomon's litter; threescore valiant men escort it, the flower of Israel. They all hold swords, being skilled in war: every man's sword is ready at his side against the terrors of the night.

SONG of SONGS WHICH IS SOLOMON'S

KING SOLOMON is carried in a palanquin made for him of cypress wood brought from far Lebanon. He has had the columns thereof made of fine silver, the head-rest thereof made of gold, the seat thereof made of purple leather, and the interior walls thereof inlaid with ivory, for love of the maidens of Zion.

Go forth, O daughters of Zion and behold King Solomon wearing the crown with which his mother crowned him

ON THE DAY OF HIS WEDDING THIS DAY OF GLADNESS

IV: 1–7

S ong of Songs includes some half dozen extended passages of 100–200 words that celebrate the beloved in lavish, exuberant, and intimate physical detail. Here the young man praises the young woman. Later, in V: 10–16, she will praise him, itemizing every feature of his beautiful body. He delivers a long list of vivid images from village life, comparing her eyes to doves, her teeth to newly washed lambs, her lips to a crimson ribbon, and her breasts to twin fawns.

When calligraphers map out a long text, their first job is to help the reader decide what to look at first, second, and later. It seemed obvious here that I should focus the design on "You are perfect" and then list the ways. But the many translations of this phrase ranged from insipid to over the top to wide of the target. In the King James Bible, the lover starts off with the bland "thou art all fair" that most modern women would find underwhelming; he ends with the back-handed "There is no spot in thee." I eventually found a more elegant, eloquent translation: "You are perfect . . . there is no flaw in you." This statement, slightly rephrased, also anchors the lower corners.

Because the poem is so explicit about the woman's beautiful body, I looked for ways that the layout could suggest her presence. I framed the larger text in a curved band that resembles a necklace resting on her breasts. I decorated this semicircle in rich enamel colors to evoke the surrounding green hills, blue sky, and white clouds— the basic elements that form boundaries to the poet's world.

I chose simple Bookhand lettering to make this long description easy to read. To add visual depth to lines of small letters, I filled the pen with a different color for some of the writing. Those subtle green letters make the purple text look as though the necklace continued full circle; even the small swashes of the f in the citation are meant to look like the bow knot that fastens it at the nape of her neck. Finally, a line of tiny Italic letters reinforces and decorates the outer edge of the curve like fine filigree.

Your eyes are as doves behind your veil, and your hair is as a flock of goats, that stream down from the mountains of Gilead. Your teeth are like a flock of sheep newly shorn, which come up from the washing, of which every one bears twins, and none are unmatched. Your lips are like a ribbon of crimson, and your mouth speaks words of enchantment: your cheeks have the blush of pomegranates behind your veil. Your neck is like the tower that David built for an armory and adorned with a thousand shields, and each is the blazonry of a hero. Your breasts are like the twin fawns of a gazelle, that graze among the lilies.

Until the day breathes cool, and the shadows lengthen, I will hasten to the mountain of myrrh and the hill of frankincense.

You are perfect, MY BELOVED; there is no flaw in you.

HOW beautiful you are, O beloved;

My beloved, you are perfect; you have no flaws.

IV: 8–9

I was enchanted by these verses about a young woman who lives in the hills with lions and panthers, and the young man who hopes to coax her down. This page practically designed itself. The narrative starts in the far distance and ends up close enough to see the sparkle in her eyes and the gem in her necklace.

This layout relies on a half dozen standard visual techniques that calligraphers can borrow from landscape painters to add the illusion of a third dimension to a two-dimensional page. Things that are further away change in four predictable ways: they appear smaller, closer together, paler, and bluer. In addition, diagonals that are nearer to the viewer overlap diagonals that are farther away. And white space can suggest the mist that collects in the valleys of many mountain landscapes. (Figure IV: 8-9)

Figure IV: 8-9

The narrative begins in faraway Lebanon, crossing several mountain ranges and passing by the lairs of wild animals. To make even the most distant letters readable, I used lines of simple Bookhand, setting them at an angle to suggest mountains. I started with the smallest, palest letters, and gradually made them larger and darker. Each subsequent phrase required fewer words and larger letters than the one before, until the final line nearly filled the space. Along the way, both the imagery and the words became more personal, moving from distant hills to a single gem on a woman's neck.

Although almost every letter of the lowercase alphabet has been simplified over the centuries, Bookhand still offers an older, more complicated form of the small g, with a descender that was perfect for this design. I wanted the gem to be green, to contrast with the blue lettering and yet still evoke the outdoors. It also had to be round, to fit into the tail of the g—despite protests from several literal-minded gem experts, one of whom told me, "No one would ever give an emerald a round cut like that."

I arranged the words of the citation to imitate little light beams reflected from the facets of the gem, echoing the sparkles suggested by "one glance from your eyes."

Come away with me from Lebanon, my beloved,
my promised bride; come away from Lebanon.

Leave your hideaway in the mountain tops
of Amana, and of Senir and Hermon;

Abandon the seclusion of your
wilderness and your companions;

Leave the wild lions and
panthers who guard you.

You have ravished my
heart, O my beloved,

with one glance
from your eyes,

with one gem from
your necklace

SONG of SONGS

Chapter IV:
Verses 8-9

Which is
Solomon's

IV: 10–11

An art professor I knew at Rhode Island School of Design used to give his students an assignment he called "The Four Uglies." It required them to choose the four colors they liked least, and then compose a design that made them work together. The students, grumbling at first, eventually came to describe this experience as "a revelation," "an eye-opener," and "a life-changer."

I've taken this lesson to heart. No color is intrinsically ugly; it's all in the context. It has encouraged me to venture out of my comfort zone, to try colors I think I don't like.

Life imitates art, we know, and "The Four Uglies" can teach us lessons that are not limited to Design 101. It is a metaphor for a larger idea; many inspiring tales feature a group of difficult people, like the classic war movie "The Dirty Dozen," where the storyteller's art turns these failed characters into a team of winners by using the flaws in one to offset the needs of another. The truth is that *nobody* is a lost cause, not even the human equivalents of such "ugly" colors as puce, mud, pink, and acid yellow. In this design, they shine together as purple, umber, rose, and sunshine.

But the moral truth that can transform four discordant colors into a harmonious design, or a group of losers into a group of winners, can lead us even further beyond the virtues of teamwork, to remind us that all of us live lives full of ugly colors that we did not choose. They come in all forms, from what we are born with and what our families suffer through, to the random bad luck of the era we live in and the accidents we learn from. Experiences don't usually oblige us by arriving in our favorite color, but they may be made beautiful and meaningful in a design.

Art requires contrast. Painters have to use dark paint as well as bright colors. Music needs dissonance to balance its harmony. Drama must have disruption to find resolution. Words can be written, and read, in almost any combination of colors. These insights can help people appreciate how even the ugliest elements can come together somehow to form a beautiful whole.

How delicious is your love, O my beloved,

Sweet is

sweeter than the finest rare wine. And the

every word from

aroma of your perfume is richer than the

your lips,

most exquisite spices. Your kisses

my beloved,

taste of honeycomb, O my beloved; every

and your kisses

word from your lips is honey and cream.

taste of honey

Your garments breathe out the scent of the

and cream.

outdoors, of the wild mountain heights.

SONG *of* SONGS IV: 10~11
Which is Solomon's

IV: 12–15

Aperennial problem of biblical translation can be seen here in the invocation "my sister, my spouse" from the King James Version. It's clearly not what it sounds like to modern ears. In fact, Jewish law prohibits marriage between close relatives and in-laws. Scholars agree that the poet's original intent was to suggest not incest, but familial tenderness.

Of course today's reader can figure out that "my sister" is just an archaic term of affection, the way we call someone "baby" or refer to a good friend as "brother." But it is distracting, and it distances us from Scripture that otherwise sounds fresh and engaging. Many modern translators take the initiative by substituting fond terms like "my darling" or referring to her as "my bride." In any translation, there is often a trade-off between staying faithful to the original word and making sense in present-day speech. I chose "my beloved" for both sexes.

The poet's image of a walled garden made this layout easy to design. After creating walls of hedge from blocks of text, I changed a few letters along the inner edges from parched desert brown to the blue of "a fresh spring of living water" and the green of growing plants. The little curled-up vine at the center encloses a world of its own.

Calligraphers make a lot of small changes to improve the reading experience of their viewers. Although at first I planned the upper and lower headlines to read "A GARDEN ENCLOSED . . . IS MY BELOVED," they seemed too wordy. I shortened them to "A GARDEN . . . ENCLOSED." It's simpler to read, allows for larger letters, and makes the viewer curious to find out what the garden encloses.

I searched dictionaries and translations to find out equivalents for the poet's nard, frankincense, camphire, and calamus. It is easier for the modern reader to imagine the aromas of more familiar plant names such as musk, saffron, lavender, cinnamon, and aloes.

I have to confess I cannot always resist temptation; I filled the little o's with orange to suggest fruit or flowers, simply because I like filling o's. A sharp-eyed reader can find filled-in o's in half a dozen other designs.

A GARDEN

A garden enclosed is my beloved, a pure and secret spring locked up, a fountain sealed away.

Her orchards blossom with pomegranates and the most exquisite fruits: henna and musk root; lavender and sweet green rushes; saffron and cinnamon; myrrh and aloes.

She is as a fresh spring of living water, like unto the sparkling streams that flow out of Lebanon.

Her trees are heavy laden with the honeyed spice of incense, that breathes forth its sweet fragrance.

ENCLOSED

SONG *of* SONGS   IV: 12 ~ 15

Which is Solomon's

IV: 16

Modern calligraphers who like their letter forms to look old—but not "olde"—often rely on the elegant late-medieval capitals called Versals. They can be made plainer or more ornate, and they can be used one at a time or together in words. They are easy to read, and they carry only the faintest flavor of old manuscripts. And even then, looking medieval doesn't have to mean *acting* medieval.

Conventional rules of page design used to dictate that only the first letter in the first word of a sentence or a paragraph was suitable for decorating. Calligraphy today has moved far beyond that restriction, offering freedom to decide which letter to capitalize and where to put it. Though this passage is only a single verse, it contains three distinct sections: summoning the winds to spread a garden's fragrance, describing the delights of the garden, and declaring that the lovers will enter this garden. I read the text aloud many times, listening for the main idea, and eventually found it near the end in "My beloved will enter this garden with me." I needed the reader to read that first.

To guide the eye, I reduced contrast in all the other letters and then put the crucial text in the middle of the garden hedges. I dramatized it with a bright red capital. I had chosen a translation that started with "My beloved" rather than "Let my beloved . . ." partly because a Versal M looks more like a flower than a Versal L does.

To keep the whole page unified in style, I layered lines of purple Versals onto the garden hedges. The extra ornamental strokes and lower contrast make the viewer more likely to read them later, after the simpler letters inside. And, because I like to use images that I see in my daily life, the hedges around this garden are ornamented with the kind of wrought-iron fence palings painted gold, with ornamental corners, that I walk past every morning on my way to my studio.

I kept the formal, archaic pronouns "Wake thou . . ." and "rise thou . . ." to emphasize that the speaker is addressing the invisible, super-human spirits of the wind. Ordinary pronouns sounded too casual.

Wake thou, O North Wind! and rise thou, O South Wind!

SONG of SONGS
Which is Solomon's

WE SHALL TASTE ITS EXQUISITE FRUITS

My beloved will enter this garden with me;

chapter IV
verse 16

Breathe over my garden, to spread its abroad its sweet fragrance.

V: 1

Letters are a lot like people. Some of them argue with the calligrapher every step of the way, while others are so eager to cooperate that they almost design the page themselves. This verse is made of such team players. With the crucial word "garden" at its center, the very first sentence in this verse obligingly transforms itself into an arch, making it easy for the viewer to both see it as a beckoning gateway and read it as an invitation to an outdoor party.

I formed the arch out of simple brown Roman capitals, with a rounded letter E to soften their solemnity. Though the speaker starts by greeting his beloved, "My dearest, my own," he immediately reaches out to invite friends and family to join them. In the smaller blue words twined around the arch, the poet appeals vividly to taste and smell. He describes the generous scale of the banquet by using a common poetic device from early Hebrew and nearby languages during this era; "the honeycomb and its honey" and "the milk and the wine" signify a lavish banquet. Called *parallelism*, this repetition functions like the English metaphors for abundance, "from soup to nuts," or "from head to toe."

Figure V:1

A few words needed updating, such as the phrase from the King James Version where the host calls his beloved "my sister, my spouse." To avoid distracting the reader, today's translations employ less loaded terms such as "my dearest," "my own," "my equal," "my treasure."

This feast seems to celebrate a betrothal or wedding. I used memories from several recent outdoor weddings to recreate the festive mood of being elegantly dressed but relaxing outdoors in a garden. I piled green branches onto the top of the arch and let them trail below. By lettering the citation under the arch in tiny gray letters, I created a hint of the filmy drapery that decorates so many weddings. The image also suggests the way a bride's face can be crowned by vines and framed by a soft translucent veil. (Figure V: 1)

I HAVE COME INTO OUR GARDEN, MY DEAREST, MY OWN

I have eaten the honeycomb and its honey; I have drunk the milk and the wine;

I have eaten the honeycomb and its honey;

and the spices;

I have gathered the myrrh

SONG of SONGS

Chapter Five:

Which is Solomon's

Verse One

Feast, my friends;

and drink your fill of love.

V: 2–6

Calligraphers, though they use traditional letterforms, don't have to arrange them in antiquated page designs. Art should always reflect an artist's world. Music, painting, dance, and poetry are at their most compelling when their creators express ideas from their own era.

I wanted to contrast two powerful, incompatible ideas from these verses: heat versus cold, intimacy versus loneliness, eager anticipation versus bleak despair. The image that sprang to mind was a small crucible of incandescent human emotion at the center of a vast nighttime sky, the kind of image now coming back to earth every day from orbiting telescopes and planetary probes. I didn't have to settle for a quaint medieval view of the cosmos (Figure V: 2-6, a) when I could choose from awe-inspiring images of Saturn's rings, exploding novas, whirling galaxies, and interstellar clouds. (Figure V: 2-6, b)

Figure V:2-6 a

Figure V:2-6 b

After all, Song of Songs is about timeless human truths, framed in imagery that does not pin them to one particular age. Modern photographs from deep in space need not take the mystery out of the universe or diminish one's spiritual vision. I welcomed the chance to base my design on these spectacular new ways of visualizing our world in the universe.

The first verses set the scene, as the young woman's lover comes to her bedroom door and she lets him in with joyous anticipation. The focus of the poem is the surge of overwhelming physical arousal at her very core, felt with red-hot intensity and described in graphic detail. Then he is gone, without even the echo of a farewell.

To suggest the spectrum of her emotions, I let the lines of lettering spiral inward to the words "WITHIN ME" at the glowing center of the vortex, then unwind back outward into the infinite dark and cold of space, as the moment passes and the young woman waits, alone.

Look closely and you will see hundreds of stars that seem to form iconic patterns of double helix, twisted cord, spiral, and sine wave, between the whirling arms of the galaxy that a young woman's words have created.

O
tell us:
how is your beloved
so different from all others,
that you should want us to praise him too?

My beloved is fearless and handsome; truly he is a paragon among ten thousand other men! His head is purest gold, his wavy hair is black like a raven. His eyes sparkle like two twinned doves bathed in milk and glowing like opals about the rim of a fountain. His cheeks are like gardens of sweet spices, ever giving off a rich fragrance. His lips are like flowering lilies, honeyed with the scent of myrrh. His arms are like rounded ingots of gold, set with beryl. His body is like a work of the brightest ivory, graced with gems of lapis lazuli. His legs stand like columns of fine alabaster, set on a base of gold. His bearing is stately, like the noble cedars of Lebanon.

The words of his mouth are sweetness itself and he is desirable to me in every way.

MY BELOVED
is beyond compare
among ten
thousand
men!

SONG of SONGS,

Which is Solomon's

Chapter V: Verses 9–16

These
are the virtues
of him who is my
beloved and my friend;

So he
outshines
all others, O ye
daughters of Zion.

VI: 1–3

In these three verses, the young woman's friends ask her playfully, in Italic script, where her lover is, and offer to help her find him. In simple, sincere Bookhand, she answers them that he is "in our garden," grazing his sheep among her lilies, thus painting a provocative word picture of their intimacy. In small Roman capitals, at the very center, she recites a vow of their commitment to each other. The lilies enclose the whole text.

When I began to arrange the first four short phrases, I was struck by how much the plan of a whole garden echoes a single flower. The purple and orange quarters look like petals with orange centers, but at the same time they resemble beds of contrasting flowers with formal paths between them. I arranged the declaration of love as if it were an inscription carved on slate at the center of the garden.

With the garden mapped out in flowerbeds, I looked for a way to render the lilies themselves. The words of the citation divided equally into four sides of a square. Because Gothic's repeated verticals look so much like flower stems, I used green Gothic letters to write them; I exaggerated the ascenders and descenders of f, h, l, and p, and shaped the swashes of s and t and capital S and V to look like leaves and flowers. In addition, I compressed the verticals, making the letters extra tall and extra narrow, to encourage the viewer to see them as a row of lilies. I like to use Gothic calligraphy to serve a higher purpose than its timeworn association with diplomas and Victorian Christmas cards. Its tight spacing can encourage people to *see* it as an image first and only *read* it as words later.

I further strengthened the likeness of Gothic letters to lilies by shaping their curved swashes to look like flowers and leaves, then shading them with pale color. Although I was tempted by the wide range of lily colors, from deep purple-brown to orange-red to softest coral, I ended up making it easy to recognize the letters as lilies by painting their tips a pale green and adding powdery yellow spathes to their centers.

Song of Songs which is Solomon

Chapter Six · Verses 1-3

Where has your beloved gone, O most beautiful among all women? Where is he?

My beloved has gone down by our garden, to the beds of spice.

YOU ARE MINE, O BELOVED, AND I AM YOURS

There he pastures his flocks; they graze among my fragrant lilies.

Tell us where your beloved has gone so that we may help you to search for him.

VI: 4–7

Some letters feel at home anywhere. Medieval Versals are readable at all sizes, from the quarter-inch capital in a tiny Book of Hours (Figure VI: 4-7, a) to the three-inch ornamented capital big enough for a choir to read at a distance (Figure VI: 4-7, b). They blend easily with old or modern letter styles. They can be decorated or left plain. They are formal enough to add dignity when used one by one, but simple enough to be readable in whole words.

When I began to study calligraphy, I realized that Versals had already inscribed themselves in my memory ten years before. Early visual images mean a lot to artists. Without being aware of it, I'd been thinking about Versals since 1955, when I first met them in the Revised Standard

Figure V:4-7 a, b

Bible that I was awarded for singing in the youth choir at Collegiate Presbyterian Church in Ames, Iowa. Although its black and white typeset pages of Scripture were virtually unadorned (see II: 1-2, page 36), an enterprising mid-twentieth-century designer had embellished its presentation page with a red and blue border, a large initial, thin lead lines of red, and whole words made of bright blue Versals (Figure VI: 4-7, c). I was hooked.

Figure V:4-7 c

Versals helped me reconcile two worlds in this design: the permanence of the night sky overhead and the immediacy of familiar sights in the village. The words of praise are rendered in warm images from everyday life, comparing the beloved's rippling hair to a herd of goats, her white teeth to newly washed twin lambs, and her pink cheeks to pomegranate halves. In contrast with these intimate, earthy images, the phrase "Majestic as the starry midnight sky" arches overhead. To give it extra gravitas, I rendered it in dark purple Versals on an arc that appears to be part of a huge circle. A background of star maps—vaguely suggesting a Zodiac—evokes the passage of time. A variety of other curves seems to trace the orbits of other worlds, from other skies.

YOU ARE LOVELY AS THE CITY OF TIRZAH, ENCHANTING AS JERUSALEM

MAJESTIC AS THE

STARRY MIDNIGHT SKY

Turn your eyes away, for with a single glance they cast a spell on me!

O
beloved,
your hair is
like a flock of goats that
stream down from the heights of Mount Gilead.
Your teeth are like a flock of the whitest sheep,
which come up freshly washed for shearing from
the spring, whereof every one has borne twin
lambs; and not one is missing or unmatched.
The curve of your cheek has the soft blush of
pomegranate halves behind the veil of your hair.

VI: 8–10

The speaker goes into extravagant detail here, boasting about how his beloved is superior to the king's many queens and concubines, to her mother's other children, and even to the sun and moon, adding that her friends all praise her. I wanted to dramatize this image of how, in his eyes, she outshines everyone and everything around her.

My main choice was between metaphors of the sun or moon. Throughout Song of Songs, the young woman's voice has been balanced, mature, and poised, and in this passage she is seen through the eyes of others, who openly admire her. That reflected praise made her seem more like the softly glowing moon than the brightly shining noonday sun. I felt that "luminous" suited her better than "dazzling." Using letters only, I built up a complex design that combined a full moon, moonbeams, a moon-dog, and intersecting rays. Because the text was more than 100 words long, I needed to break it into several sections and decide their sequence. Although the comparison to Solomon's many queens and concubines is flattering, I felt that the reader did not need to read it first—the main point is the superlative beauty of the beloved, not the number of wives in King Solomon's harem.

I lettered the central disc of the moon's surface with simple soft blue Roman capitals. The many O's reminded me of lunar craters. The beams that fall around and over the moon are also made of letters, either stacked in narrow columns or slanted along an angled line. This wide stripe of gray text passes right through the central blue capitals where it crosses the moon, and yet it does not lose readability. In a subtle detail, a contrasting color falls diagonally through the gray band like a slender golden moonbeam.

In this design, pen strokes make virtually every bit of color on the page. Even the decorative circles that halo the moon are built up of the zigzag flourishes that were wildly popular with calligraphers in the eighteenth and nineteenth centuries.

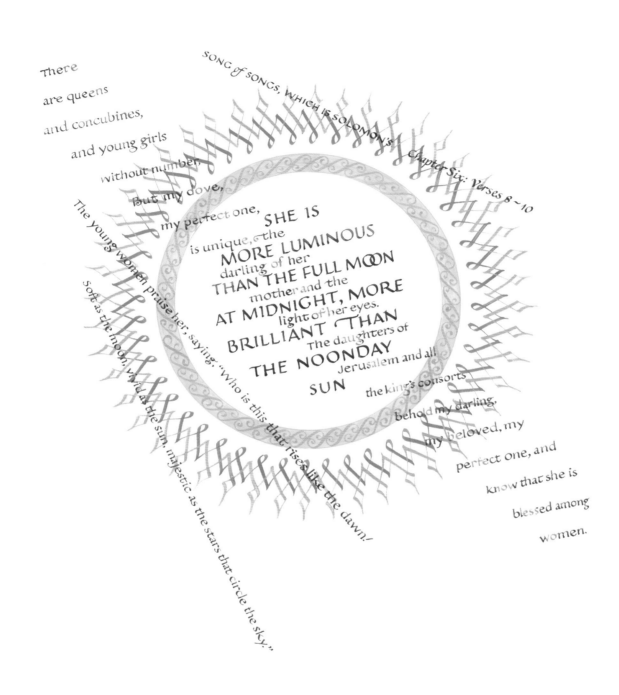

There

are queens

and concubines,

and young girls

without number,

But my dove,

my perfect one,

is unique, the

darling of her

mother and the

light of her eyes.

The daughters of

Jerusalem and all

the king's consorts

behold my darling,

my beloved, my

perfect one, and

know that she is

blessed among

women.

SONG of SONGS, WHICH IS SOLOMON'S · Chapter Six: Verses 8 ~ 10

The young women praise her, saying: "who is this that rises like the dawn!

Soft as the moon, wild as the sun, majestic as the stars that circle the sky."

SHE IS
MORE LUMINOUS
THAN THE FULL MOON
AT MIDNIGHT, MORE
BRILLIANT THAN
THE NOONDAY
SUN

VI: 11–12

Although these verses are short and most of the words are easy to translate, they are, according to poet and scholar Chana Bloch, "generally conceded to be the most difficult verse in the Song." Different versions differ widely. The problem is not the words themselves, but the figure of speech that starts the second verse with an abrupt shift. It means something like, "Before I knew what was happening, I found myself riding in a chariot." It may be an image that comes from a neighboring country's poetic tradition. The chariot itself may symbolize worldly or spiritual power, and the nut trees may invoke fertility. Scholars disagree too about whether more than one person is speaking, or whose voice it is.

I had to choose among these interpretations to find the one that made sense to me. I pictured the kind of daydreamer who can start out gardening in the back yard and end up in the clouds.

This is just one of many passages in Song of Solomon where the design helps reconcile two opposing ideas. The first verse describes the real world of orchard gardening, where leaves and buds and blossoms must be checked and tended every day. The colors and the long ascenders reinforce this idea. Careful readers may notice that a soft lilac tint fills the center of each O to suggest fruits and flowers.

The second verse then suddenly lurches from the orchards and vineyards into a fantasy land, where together the lovers ride in a royal chariot and reign over an imaginary kingdom. The gray line of the citation meanders along the gap between these two worlds.

Calligraphy changes the imaginary tone of voice by changing the style, size, color, or spacing of letters on the page. Here, I lettered the verse about the real world in plain green Bookhand and the verse about the daydream in elegant purple Italic; the two swashed letters T and h impersonate a regal couple standing side by side. I kept both scripts the same size, however, to show that both worlds seem equally real to the speaker. A blue color shift within both verses adds extra depth by suggesting a path that leads from one world to the other.

I walked down to the orchard
where almond trees blossom,
to look for buds on the vines,
and for pomegranates in
flower.

SONG of SONGS, which is Solomon's. Chapter Six: verses 11 ~ 12

Then
suddenly, in my daydreams,
I rode in a chariot beside my prince,
AND I HELD DOMINION
OVER ALL THAT I SAW.

VI: 13

This single verse about a dancer presents several puzzles. The text compares her to two armies meeting, a difficult metaphor that puzzles readers and challenges translators. Nor can they agree about the origin of her name. The onlookers call her the Shulamite, a term that scholars politely describe as "disputed." Its sound suggests Solomon, Jerusalem, or Shalom. It may refer to an ancient war goddess; she may come from a now-forgotten city. Some scholarly studies devote pages to the debate over this name, which appears only once in the Bible.

In the first phrase, the spectators call out to the dancer and urge her to keep dancing. Then they describe how her dancing delights their eyes. In the final sentence, they encourage her again. I found two ways to start the central phrase: "We gaze at her while she dances" or "She dances while we gaze." I chose a word order that centers on the woman rather than the people who watch her, making her the subject rather than the object. I should also confess that as a calligrapher I wanted to put S rather than W at the beginning of that sentence, to emphasize the sinuous image. Whenever I have a choice, I like to capitalize a letter that will reinforce my design.

The dancer is described mainly by the way she moves, not how she looks. The margins of the text flex in an S shape, while the lines of lettering themselves stay level. Those "two armies" of some translators could just as well be the two "lines of dancers" preferred by others. She might be the soloist, or simply a favorite taking her turn at pirouetting down the path between her friends. The contours form a winding curve, and the green swash seems to follow a pivot point on her moving body.

To choose colors, I looked at many costume designs from operas, movies, paintings, and ballets where village dancers play a part. I made the letter strokes longer and added extra swashes, to evoke the handmade tassels, ribbons, fringe, and scarves in simple colors that flutter from the costumes and move when the dancer moves.

O MAIDEN of SHULAM,

SHE DANCES

WE LOVE to watch you as you turn and then return, O graceful dancer.

WHILE WE GAZE on HER TURNING BETWEEN THE LINES of DANCERS

Turn and return again, to delight our eyes once more.

SONG of SONGS VI: 13
Which is Solomon's

VII: 1–6

I n these verses a young man praises the exquisite physical beauty of the young woman he loves, starting with a glimpse of her feet. As his gaze moves upward, he describes each part of her body with a voluptuous metaphor: golden wheat, twin gazelle fawns, a rounded goblet, and starlit reflecting pools.

Rather than illustrating these comparisons literally, I wanted a design that would imply some of the sensations they inspire. The most striking poetic image was about her eyes, which one translator rendered as prosaic "fishpools" but which I preferred to imagine glimmering "like two reflecting pools of starry light." I looked for a repeating pattern that could spread outward from the center like sparkling ripples.

I first chose a basic shape, as I had done with the four other long poems of physical praise. This octagonal motif calls to mind the intricate tilework found throughout the Mediterranean world, evoking a cool surface in a hot climate. The color scheme of royal blue, verdigris, and amber repeats the idea by writing the key phrase onto the border of the octagonal figure itself, in a swashed lettering style that is abstract enough to look like decoration at first glance. To reinforce the idea of ripples, I laid down a thin line that echoes the grout between tiles, and let it repeat outward in parallel until it seemed to wash against the bottom line. The gouache ink suggests the powdery matte surface of grout (Figure VII: 1-7). It's too pale to be the first thing you see, but once you see it, it makes the page feel richer.

Calligraphy can aspire to many of the virtues of fine art: texture, color value, composition, proportion, and symbolism. Like a book that you return to several times in your life, or the concerto you enjoy more on each hearing, a page of calligraphy can encourage both calligrapher and viewer not to stop with one encounter. By adding depth with details like this faint geometric background grid, I like to reward viewers who take the time to look again.

Figure VII: 1-7

Your naked feet are exquisite, glimpsed through your sandals;
Your graceful thighs are like fine jewelry, shaped by an artist's hand.
Your navel is a rounded goblet, ever filled with true intoxication;
Your waist is a silken sheaf of golden wheat, encircled by lilies.
Your breasts are like little deer, like unto twin fawns of a gazelle.
Your neck is like a tower curved and slender, fashioned of ivory.
Your eyes glimmer like two reflecting pools of starry light;
Your nose is shapely, like a proud monument from Damascus.
Your head crowns you like Mount Carmel, and your hair shines
in the sun's light; in its tresses a king could be held captivated.

YOU ARE ENCHANTING IN EVERY WAY, O BELOVED

Your eyes glimmer like two reflecting pools of starry light.

VII: 6–10

This design is based on a flexible, accommodating layout that helps to coordinate different line lengths into a unified design. I spent a lot of time with penciling and erasing, to help the lines guide the reader's eye. I did not try to force the layout into a literal diagram of a palm trunk, but aimed instead to create a generalized image of sturdy and fruitful growth. Color supported this metaphor by infusing the warm golden ochre with purple shadows.

Once I finished lettering the text, it felt overwhelmed by the space around it. I framed it with lines of the citation, arranging them to reinforce the corners with decorative scrollwork.

As a matter of courtesy and professionalism, I make it a rule to include a citation *every time* I letter anyone else's words. Formal references are obligatory in academia, to establish that the text you are quoting is a real source and not something you just made up. Non-academic authors still have to give credit when they borrow another author's words. Calligraphers, too, should maintain a high standard. Now that the internet makes it so easy to check, there's no excuse for shrugging off a hand-lettered quote as "anonymous" or taking a stab at who you think you remember wrote it and where you might have read it. For instance, Humphrey Bogart did not actually say "Play it again, Sam" in *Casablanca*. Nor did Winston Churchill promise "Blood, sweat, and tears."

Biblical citations should lead the reader to the right book, at least, no matter how short the verse or how loose the translation. Finding the original citation also makes you check the wording. Dozens of popular Bible verses turn out to have been penned by Shakespeare—and vice versa.

Calligraphers have to be meticulous about the accuracy of their text partly because errors are always waiting to creep in. Calligraphy pens can be as treacherous as human memory. The medieval scriptorium recognized that the pen can make its own errors, and it enforced strict rules to prevent the kind of distractions that would lead their monkish copyists to make mistakes. Still, people will forgive slips of the pen much more readily than slipshod shortcuts.

How
beautiful
you are to me,

O my love and my delight, and how happy you make me!

Like a noble palm tree you stand shapely and tall for me to climb;

your breasts feel like clusters of ripening grapes for me to caress;

your breath evokes the exquisite scent of sweet pomegranates;

Your lips taste like the most fragrant wine that glides smoothly under the roof of your mouth and over your tongue

so that even now while you lie slumbering deep in dreams,

your voice still whispers to me with soft words of love.

O my beloved, we long only for each other.

VII: 11–13

This design uses a rich palette of brown vines, green leaves, and purple grapes to celebrate a successful harvest, heaping them in abundance over the doorway. It is a universal image, but it can also suggest the little outdoor shed that observant Jews construct to eat and sleep in during the one-week harvest holiday of Sukkot. This sense of plenty infuses the words of the lovers, who describe their plans to spend the coming night, and implicitly the rest of their lives, outdoors together.

The first and last verses cooperated with my plan to make them into a door frame, even letting me finish both columns with the same two words, "my love." This design obligingly freed up the middle verse to form the vines, with its first three words forming an extra lintel above. It wasn't obvious, however, which letter of that headline I ought to capitalize. I have learned not to default automatically to the first letter of any quotation, but to sift through it to find a less obvious, more engaging choice. My other Song of Songs designs had given me a lot of capital O's already, nor would the B of "beloved" have added much meaning to the design. I ultimately enlarged V, near the end of "beloved," letting it echo the shape of the grape bunches below. I sank it below the other letters, to imply the weight of a grape bunch. I avoided being too realistic; I just hinted at the color of grapes, added white dots to evoke highlights, and used a few small curlicues to suggest twining tendrils.

Calligraphy constantly offers the adventurous artist new ways to innovate on the page, by deciding what to include and what to omit. I was inspired as a teenager by the poetry of E. E. Cummings, who disregarded the conventional rules of typesetting. Many of his poems show how much it matters which letters you choose to capitalize and where you decide to place them on the page, to help readers hear the poet's voice in their heads. Poet, painter, and preacher's kid, he blazed a path for artists in any medium to follow.

O MY BELOVED

Let us go to the vineyard at dawn;
To see if bud and blossom are on the grapevine
and if the pomegranate is in flower;

Come, my love, let us go out into the fields; let us lie all night together among the flowering henna. There will I give you the gift of my love.

The scent of mandrake fills the air. And our doorway is crowned with all the rarest fruits, both fresh and mellowed, which I have kept for you, my love.

Chapter VII:

SONG of SONGS

Which is Solomon's

Verses 11~13

VIII: 1–3

In this design, calligraphy maps the emotional boundary between inner passion and outward restraint. The text begins with a young woman yearning to kiss her beloved in public, the way she could express her affection to a brother. It goes on to describe her wanting to take him home and share sweet wine with him, and it ends with her anticipation of being folded in his arms and making passionate love.

The first and second verse form two columns that are balanced and calm, like the security of her childhood home. The saturated ink color shifts from purple letters to red and back, and the same red letters bracket the oval at top and bottom, reinforcing the page's symmetry.

The young woman describes an outer world where she has to behave with modesty, contrasting it with the world inside her walls where she and her lover are free to let their feelings show. The oval frame represents this divide: its hard exterior is spiky and bright, keeping the rest of the text at bay, while its lining is made up of soft silver curlicues.

The third verse, safe inside the silver frame, describes in sensuous detail exactly how her lover's arms will hold her. The stylized phrases repeat almost verbatim the words of II: 6 and are thought by scholars to be a common poetic construction from neighboring countries of the era 600 BCE. The powdery blue Italic letters, gracefully swashed, echo the soft silver coils and contrast with the hard little green gems. Only inside these walls, protected from public disapproval, can the lovers be their true selves, rather than staying at the distance required by public approval.

Figure VIII 1-3

Artists use—and maybe overuse—the motto "I paint what I see," but in this design I really did. I look at this ring (Figure VIII: 1-3) every day as I write, type, and paint. It is part of my landscape. When I needed to portray the visual contrast between hard and soft, I contrasted the light that bounces off diamonds to the light that is captured by an opal.

SONG
of SONGS
Which is Solomon's

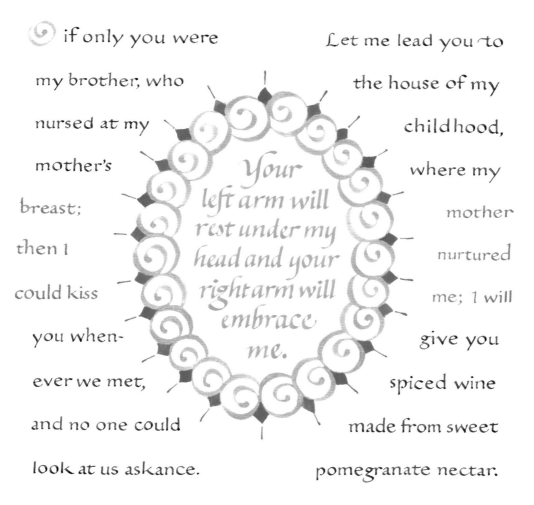

if only you were
my brother, who
nursed at my
mother's
breast;
then I
could kiss
you when-
ever we met,
and no one could
look at us askance.

Let me lead you to
the house of my
childhood,
where my
mother
nurtured
me; I will
give you
spiced wine
made from sweet
pomegranate nectar.

Your left arm will rest under my head and your right arm will embrace me.

Chapter Eight:
Verses
1~3

VIII: 4

I n this verse, the young woman speaks to her friends, the "daughters of Jerusalem," entreating them to be cautious about love. It will grow and mature, but only if the lovers use caution and do not rush it. I chose the growing plant (Figures VIII: 4, a, b, c) as my own visual metaphor for the love described in these verses.

Figures VIII: 4 a, b, c

This is again that verse that is thrice repeated almost verbatim. It brackets the book, appearing twice near the beginning and once near the end.

The third design in this series shows the plant in its prime, leafed out and firmly rooted. Although this final text is shorter by half (it omits the oath about wild deer and gazelles), its remaining words fill the page with branches, leaves, roots, and the very soil that holds it up. Grounded in horizontal lines of sturdy brown lettering, the young woman's words sound content and self-confident. She has exercised restraint and now her love has come of age.

I was curious, all the way along, about how the voice can seem so sure of this need for slow growth. She seems to speak from experience; it is she who cautions the chorus rather than the other way around. While elsewhere she seems almost unable to master her feelings of obsession and physical desire, here she has a level head and a firm tone of voice that claims control of the situation. She is not one of those sadder but wiser heroines of cautionary love stories or a helpless victim of other people's impulses, as her brothers fear. Although she is presumably still very young, she already knows what will keep love safe and strong as it ripens—and what will not.

O daughters of Jerusalem, I caution you,

Stir not up nor arouse love, before it has ripened.

SONG of SONGS, Which is Solomon's, Chapter Eight: Verse 4

VIII: 5

Because letters are mainly empty space, one of the perennial challenges of calligraphy is how to get more color onto the page. Because I like my designs to rely mainly on letters, I am reluctant to add the colorful pictures, ornaments, and borders that might compete with the simple beauty of the written words. This means that I rely on half a dozen other strategies to add color: make the letters heavier; move them closer together; use more saturated ink colors; and add extra pen strokes of color between the lines of lettering, the words, the letters, or inside the letters themselves.

The very best way to add color to the page, however, is to inspire the readers to put it there themselves. The colors they imagine are always richer than those the artist can lay on the page, the same way that what happens offstage in a Greek play is always more dramatic than what the audience can see, and horror movies are always more disturbing when you can't actually see the monster. The imagery in this text is clear and familiar. There is no need to draw a picture of an apricot tree when the letters themselves can create the illusion of brown branches, green leaves, and orange apricots.

I first arranged the main lines of lettering to suggest branches. The brown lines arch and zigzag just slightly, but not enough to disrupt a smooth reading. The leaf-shaped swashes that grow out of the branches are as dark as the bark itself, so as not to distract from the words. The citation also reinforces the leaf shape suggested by the swash on I. And the filled O's preview the ripe apricot that hangs below.

I made the large apricot out of letters in two lush shades of orange that I underlined to intensify the color. I thought that the round fruit might seem more enticing if I let the viewer look inside it to see the rich brown sliver of its hidden seed. Accentuating the axis of the round fruit also let me make it obvious that it is not hanging immobile, but it has swung about twenty degrees off vertical, to suggest that a breeze, or a pair of lovers, recently brushed by.

Who is this coming up out of the wilderness, leaning on the shoulder of her beloved?

VIII: 5

SONG of SONGS
Which is Solomon's

I found you and awakened you to love beneath the apricot tree, the very tree where your mother conceived you and gave birth to you.

English speakers have freely used the phrase "green with envy" for 400 years. Anyone who has ever felt envy, however, can confirm that jealousy feels much more like the fierce red embers of these verses, not only in its heat but in the way it is always ready to flare back up into a raging fire. The fire of envy made the color choice easy for this design: intense shades of red, orange, and yellow, flanking a central column of calmer dark purple and smoky blue. I made gashes of color between lines of lettering using a handmade pen nib that could be made to scrape fitfully along the paper, splattering when it snags. The underlying heat seems to break out here and there at the tops of the tall letters.

The central column establishes the idea that love can guard against the ravages of envy, like a ritual seal bound over the heart or on the arm. The largest lines of lettering create an image of overlapping strips held together by a flat round signet (Figure VIII: 6-7, a). I chose the cool gray-blue color of the signet specifically to contrast with the hot colors of the embers. Such seals have been added to written documents, in both East and West, for thousands of years. They formalize a contractual promise, and they imply that it is backed up by a ruling authority that will enforce it.

This design relies on tight control of the line length. By overlapping N with E and H with E, I let each of the large purple words fill one line, except for the words "As a," which I shoehorned into the space using a time-honored tactic known to scribes for 2,000 years. Roman carvers often shrank some letters of an inscription to make it fit the space (Figure VIII: 6-7, b). Medieval scribes, too, often substituted tiny abbreviations or just pushed two letters together to fit into the space of one and a half, forming a ligature like "do" in "domos" (Figure VIII: 6-7, c).

Figure VIII 6-7 a

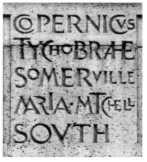

Figure VIII 6-7 b

Figure VIII 6-7 c

SONG *of* SONGS
Which is Solomon's

THE DEEPEST OF OCEANS

BIND

CANNOT EXTINGUISH LOVE,

For love
is strong as
death;
jealousy
is cruel as
the grave;

ME AS A

NOR CAN A RIVER DROWN IT;

SIGNET

IF A MAN TRIED

set me as a seal · up on your arm

OVER

TO BUY LOVE WITH

Even its embers
are coals of
fire, which
ignite a most
ravenous
flame.

YOUR

ALL THE GOLD OF HIS HOUSE,

HEART

HE WOULD BE UTTERLY DESPISED.

VIII: 6 ~ 7

VIII: 8–9

In this chapter, we finally hear from the young woman's brothers, who were first mentioned in Chapter I: 5–6, where they forced her to work in the fields. In these verses, she is confined in a rectangle formed by the words of their worry. They have ambivalent feelings about her, and they cannot decide whether she is at risk and how. Is she resisting improper advances or is she attracting them? Is she in more danger from the men around her or from her own impulses?

Where the brothers declare that their little sister "hath no breasts," I have chosen a kinder, less clinical translation than the King James Version. Their concern is not specifically about her breasts, which are just an index of how ready she is for marriage. The brothers really mean that while she is physically not quite ready for marriage, she is nevertheless still vulnerable to seduction. That's what they worry about; they are responsible for finding her a husband, and any mistakes will hurt her and damage the whole family.

They describe their sister as a fortress. In this metaphor, any existing wall—her virtue and strength—should be reinforced and made taller, and any open doorway—her vulnerability and weakness—should be boarded up. They celebrate and value her, since a marriageable sister will connect their family to others, but they also fear for her and fence her in. They want to encourage her modesty while they protect her against her own vulnerability. Even the layout reinforces this difference, placing the rampart above and the barricade below.

I lettered the brothers' rhetorical question in emerald green, using hard-edged, legalistic Gothic letters to give the voices a preachy overtone. The smaller words in purple, about making walls higher and boarding up doors, tightly bracket the larger words. The layout, with its formal crown and ornamental base of golden ochre, evokes a precious ritual object both protected and imprisoned in a frame.

The decorative panels flanking the rectangle are meant to suggest family insignias. Since she does not know what family she will marry into, these banners are currently blank and generic, but their vinery adds an image of ripening fruit.

Our
little sister is
too young to wed;

if she be a wall, we will crown her with silver ramparts;

How can we protect our sister until she is safely married?

But if she be a door, we will barricade her with cedar planks.

SONG *of* SONGS
Which is Solomon's
VIII: 8-9

VIII: 10

This verse is the young woman's reply to her brothers when they fret about her chastity. She doesn't try to contradict them, admitting candidly that she knows she is desirable. Instead she declares calmly to them and to the world that she is determined to make a success of her marriage.

The design lets a warm maternal hearth outshine the insubstantial lines of worry, giving off warmth and light for those around it. To show the *idea* of fire, though, I had to look at a lot of flames. People have their own shorthand for many of nature's colors, using flat black for the night sky, fuzzy orange for foxes, purple for grape bunches, and red for apples. But artists owe their viewers a fresh take on things they see every day. Trying to step outside my own color clichés, I opened my eyes and simply looked. What color *is* a fire? What is its shape?

I started with jagged calligraphic strokes of deep yellow, then bracketed them between larger, more stable orange swashes. A few flecks of green and blue add complexity. I took care not to suggest technology from a specific era, such as kerosene lamp, gas stove, match, or candle. This securely contained universal flame sits on a strong horizontal hearth made by the words that declare her fitness for marriage.

The shape, scale, and color of this domesticated fire contrast strongly with the many chaotic fires of love we have seen raging in previous verses: her hunger for kisses in I: 2, the clandestine passion of her lover's nighttime visit in V: 6 (page 73), the torchlit street violence in V: 7–8 (page 75), and the burning envy in VIII: 6–7 (page 101). Fire appears in many different forms throughout Song of Songs, but here it has found its highest role as the core of a household.

Her own confidence in herself transforms the fuss made by her brothers into smoke that just drifts away. I repeated their words from the previous verses, so that she could put them in their proper perspective as just so much smoke. Their pale gray color lets the reader hear her confident voice first and notice only later the echo of her brothers and their worries.

How can we then keep her safe until the day she marries.

Our little sister is still too young to wed;

If she be a wall, we will crown her with ramparts of silver;

But if she be a doorway, we will barricade her with planks of cedar.

I am fully of age, desirable and faithful;

Our household truly will be

a dwelling place

of peace.

SONG of SONGS, Which is Solomon's
CHAPTER EIGHT: VERSE 10

VIII: 11–13

The theme of vineyards is woven like a bright thread through the imagery of Song of Songs, enriching more than a dozen of its calligraphic designs. Vineyards serve as a backdrop for many dramas of village life: young people meet, lovers sleep outside, family members toil, everyone guards against predators, and owners reap a profit. The harvested grapes embody ripe abundance, and their wine is an essential part of many feasts, trysts, and celebrations.

Vineyards, grapes, and wine are God's gift to manuscript artists, too, who can open a treasure box of visual ornament and sensory memories. The vines themselves have long been used in real life to decorate harvest festivals. In fact, they were such a common motif in medieval manuscripts that the word "vignette" became synonymous with a small view in a decorated frame. (Figure VIII: 11-13)

Figure VIII 11-13

In these verses, two systems of vineyard management serve as complex metaphors for two kinds of love. One is tended only by its owner, while the other requires investors and caretakers. To some scholars, it suggests that a single wife of one's own is better than the upkeep of a harem. Others think it has to do with church governance. Still others think that such a dry lesson from agricultural economics scarcely belongs in this chapter, contrasting strangely with verses about passionate embraces, red-hot envy, and a little sister in danger of seduction.

This cryptic text describes two situations without choosing a favorite for the reader. So I did too. I simply drew attention to the contrast by balancing the text in two equal halves, each part laid out in straight green rows like a vineyard and decorated with a bunch of ripe grapes.

Grapes offer a rainbow of colors to choose from. While I was mapping out this design, my local grocery store had cycled through grapes of blackish purple, indigo, icy blue, crimson, and brownish red. I finally chose my two favorites—blueish purple Concord with a powdery gray bloom and pale green Muscat with a tinge of copper—and let the readers deduce their own meaning.

Solomon had a thriving vineyard,

which he entrusted to caretakers;

Each one of them invested a full

thousand silver coins for its fruit.

While you watch over the care of your vineyard,

SPEAK; 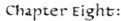 LET ME HEAR YOUR VOICE.

Your friends and I linger, longing to hear you.

SONG of SONGS

Which is Solomon's

My own vineyard lies before me,

with a thousand silver coins for

my king and only two hundred

for those who exploit its bounty.

VIII: 14

This single verse of only twenty-five words forms a satisfying finale to the chapter and the book. The verse is steeped in the colors of the setting sun and its lengthening shadows. I wanted the design to represent how it feels to turn homeward. My challenge was to build it up gradually, adding to its complexity, depth, and detail, without letting it stray in too many different directions or making it hard to read. But I did want to use calligraphy's many design tools to help the reader to get more out of it with each viewing:

❖ The five lines of lettering get closer and closer together, while they gradually darken from pale blue to indigo.

❖ The citation is set at a steep angle to suggest a falling yellow beam of light, which turns a single letter from blue to gold wherever it intersects with the main text.

❖ Intense orange and gold fill one large capital "O" to evoke the setting sun. Its light runs partway along a small arc of the earth's horizon.

❖ A halo of Gothic re-creates the legendary, elusive green flash just above the setting sun.

❖ Soft gray fills each small O to suggest pale planets or a moon.

❖ Calligraphic dots silhouette the clouds with lavender, gray, and blue.

❖ Delicate gray hairlines fall through five O's like the paths of shooting stars.

This cryptic verse creates a haunting atmosphere of silence and peace. At first I wanted to dig deeper, to pry out a more precise meaning and nail it down. Scholars and translators don't agree, however, even about such basics as whether the gazelle is imagined to be *coming* home or *going* home. Where is that home; in *here* or out *there*? Is the voice asking the beloved to go *with* me or come *to* me? Whose voice in fact is speaking: *his* or *hers*? After dozens of re-readings of dozens of translations, I couldn't decide and did not want to.

In the end, it felt right to let the whole series finish on a note of enigma. The remote and restful mood seems ready to linger long after the sun has set and Song of Songs has ended.

HASTEN TO ME, ⊙ BELOVED,

Hasten to me, O beloved,

like the gazelle or young deer

who turns homeward at dusk,

deep in the distant mountains,

where fragrant spices bloom.

Afterword

ABOUT TRANSLATION

My introduction to Song of Songs began in a Bible study class with eleven other self-conscious teenagers. Although we tried to play it cool, we were keenly interested in what these poems might be able to tell us about passionate love, and so we were disappointed to find that the biblical language kept us at arm's length from the human feelings. It skewed many of the metaphors, too, making some uncomfortably frank; some were strangely formal, and others were impossible to visualize: "my sister, my bride;" "your nose is like a tower of Lebanon." Of course, doctrine of that era explained to us that it was not love poetry at all but an allegory about God's love for us. I concluded that the language of people in love, and probably the people themselves, must have been very different in the past. It just never occurred to me that the uncertainty might be coming from the language itself.

I got reacquainted with Song of Songs a decade later when I was asked to design a wedding gift based on the popular verses I: 10–14. The same language problem cropped up immediately. The King James Version began "My beloved spake," clearly an obsolete verb form of "spoke," and continued with "the voice of the turtle," which could only make sense as "the voice of the turtledove." I was puzzled, and also put off by "thou" and "thine," but this time around I did not intend to let the old-fashioned language distract me—or my readers—from the poetry. I gathered my courage and revised those words, and I finished the design. (In fact, I was only a few years ahead of the scholarly consensus; both these updates, as well as today's pronouns "you" and "yours" would shortly make their way into the New King James Version, 1982.)

Later, in my thirties, I came across *The Complete Parallel Bible*, which lined up four translations side by side. It inspired me to try out more calligraphy designs and different verses, now that the language from Song of Songs felt like a door instead of a wall. Then just a few years ago I discovered online resources that would let me compare more than *fifty* English translations ranging from the fourteenth century to the twenty-first. What a wealth of choice! I found that I preferred austere simplicity over what C. S. Lewis dismisses as "antique glamour." After countless readings, I eventually combined all these options, choosing from more than a dozen sources to create the eclectic version shown here.

I learned that every English version of Song of Songs is derived, strictly or loosely, from the original Hebrew of some 2,500 years ago, filtered through early Greek translations of now-lost Hebrew texts. There really is no way to trace back to an original source. No manuscripts in Hebrew survive, even as fragments, from earlier than the ninth century CE, and none in Greek from before the fourth century CE. All we have are copies of copies of copies. And translations of translations of translations.

People ask me why I did not simply default to the King James Version without changes. I felt that although its translators may have been divinely inspired, they themselves were not divine; we worship the God of the Scriptures, not the Scriptures themselves. Although the King James Version was magnificent, it was not unique, since several other well-received English translations led up to it; nor was it flawless, since it needed hundreds of changes right away and thousands over the next four centuries. Dozens of new translations emerged in the twentieth century. And the English language continues to change.

A few people also question why I use any translation at all. Why not just letter the designs in Hebrew? I can only answer that like many calligraphers, I already make far too many typographic errors when I work in a language that I *do* know. Blind copying of words I can't read would multiply my typos by ten. Plus, I want to reach more viewers than only those who are fluent in Hebrew.

In a final complication all its own, Song of Songs poses a unique difficulty that casts doubt on even the most scholarly translation. There are words scattered all through the Bible that appear nowhere else; linguists call them *hapax legomenon,* classical Greek for "(a thing) being said only once." Nearly ten percent of these cryptic words occur in Song of Songs, more than in any other book of the Bible; they oblige even the most knowledgeable translator to guess at their meaning. Linguists sometimes find clues by comparing the mystery words with similar words from a different era or a related language nearby, since there is no extra context to confirm their meaning. Several recent translators helpfully describe in detail the detective work that guided their choices. Whenever I encountered a *hapax*, I felt that I was in good company, benefitting from other people's accumulated expertise but still entitled to compare their choices and use my own judgment. Ultimately, each person who reads Song of Songs in translation must accept these enigmatic words.

It is tempting for translators to simply paraphrase a difficult verse, restating in their own words what they think the Bible says. That kind of interpretation, however, lies outside the constraints of rigorous translation, and can easily slide into vanilla-flavored platitudes. Careful translators stick as close as they possibly can to the original words. Beyond that, I set myself one extra requirement: could I read this aloud to twelve teenagers in a Bible study class without making them squirm?

My goal was always to stay faithful to the Scripture while I searched for a translation that would make its meaning clear. And not just clear, but lyrical; Song of Songs must sing as well as speak. Respectful of its origin as spoken poetry, I was guided by Duke Ellington's classic advice on jazz, "If it sounds good it *is* good."

TOOLS OF TRANSLATION

I made countless small adjustments to the text, encouraged by my own minister at First Church in Boston, who reassured me that when reading Scripture aloud to a congregation, "We all do that." My goal was to make the text clear to myself first, then to my readers. I wanted to keep them from being sidetracked or confused or put off, and to enlighten them as well as delight them. Because Song of Songs does not mention the name of God or discuss doctrine, I did not think it was sacrilegious for me to search other translations for words to describe a young woman's timeless passion in the language of today.

Most of my modifications fall into the categories here:

1. UPDATING Some words are no longer in use, such as "contemned," VIII: 7, a verb derived from "contempt."

2. ART THOU? or ARE YOU? Rare and obsolete endings can distract the reader, as in "My beloved spake" from II: 10. Most of these old pronouns and verbs sound self-conscious today, though I kept them in II: 14 and IV: 16, where the poet speaks to a dove and to the winds.

3. Now TABOO In a few passages, the language implies incest, stalking, or polygamy.

4. EMPHASIZE LOCAL COLOR, DON'T EMPHASISE FOREIGN COLOUR [SIC] I used American spellings, not English.

5. HE SAID, SHE SAID While many gendered pronouns are integral to the text, some of these distinctions are not truly necessary and may distance a modern reader from the poetry.

6. KEEP A STRAIGHT FACE I rephrased double entendres whenever they struck me. If the words make the reader cringe, the design is in trouble.

7. TO ERR No document is exempt from Murphy's Law. Typos turn up everywhere, even Scripture; I had to restore a comma that I noticed missing from my own twentieth-century copy of the King James Version.

8. JUST THE WORDS The translators of the King James Version, taking their cue from the Geneva Bible of 1560, inserted numerous words to help the text make sense in English. To alert the careful reader to their additions, they had the printers set them in smaller Roman type, in contrast to Gothic. Later, after Gothic dropped out of everyday use, the added words were set in Italics to contrast with Roman lowercase. By the twentieth century, translators of other versions had dropped this custom, and so have I.

9. TELL HER ABOUT IT Many older translations describe the beloved with faint praise like "fair" or "pleasant" that sounds half-hearted today. Poetry should be vivid; modern English offers many warm and lively words of admiration.

10. A SENSE OF PLACE Many place names in Song of Songs were intended to imply luxury, strangeness, or vast distance. Although some were real and others were mythical, both kinds were familiar to readers back then. Today, however, they benefit from extra clues, such as rewording "the mountains of Bether," II: 17, to be "the mountains where fragrant spices grow."

11. LOST IN TRANSLATION Many animal and plant names in Song of Songs are unfamiliar to today's reader; I searched for modern equivalents that would evoke clearer images. For example, like many modern translators, I changed "roes," "hinds," and "harts" to "wild deer" and "gazelles."

12. BUT HOW DOES IT SOUND? Sometimes I had two equally good word choices, such as "signet" or "seal" and "cruel as the grave" or "harsh as death." But many versions of Song of Songs also included a few tone-deaf words that just grated on my ear. I re-worded some of these: "thou wert" became "you were" in VIII: 1; "the fragrance of your good ointments" became "the aroma of your perfume" in I: 3.

13. BE EXPLICIT ONLY ON PURPOSE Many words and phrases that were common in the past now sound jarringly out of place. Well-bred English speakers of the seventeenth century could refer to their bowels—even deliver a sermon about them—the way we talk about "a gut feeling." But bowels don't belong in today's love poetry. In V: 4, where the young woman describes the upheaval inside her body, every translator for the last 200 years has struggled to find a better word.

14. LET IT STAND Sometimes the language of 1611 is still the perfect choice today. Readers who know their King James Version will notice that I have lettered several of its most familiar verses virtually unchanged.

I consulted dozens of different Bibles, but even though many of them include either "new" or "standard" in their title, I had to concede that no version can claim to be final. No single translation—especially of poetry—can do more than take a photograph of a statue. It can only show a single perspective, at a single moment in time. It should motivate readers to form their own pictures of this multi-dimensional work of art.

I grew to enjoy polishing the text almost as much as I loved lettering it. Having this poetry in my eyes and ears every day for five years was a blessing and a pleasure. I wouldn't expect my readers to agree with every phrase, but I can hope they find that the translations that I chose—and the designs I shaped them into—will give them new insight.

BIBLIOGRAPHY

I began each design by reading the verses aloud from the King James Version, often turning to the Revised Standard Version to help shed light on its many old-fashioned phrases. Then I looked into a dozen more sources, digging into some early translations such as the late fourteenth-century Wycliffe Bible and The Geneva Bible from 1560. I also benefited from Chana Bloch's 1995 poetic translation, with special gratitude for her thought-provoking footnotes; I have tried to reciprocate by explaining some of my choices. Likewise, the exhaustive notes from Marvin Pope's 1977 translation linked Song of Songs to other eras, cultures, and countries, while Robert Alter's lucid 2015 translation added some of the latest scholarly insights.

Online, I found that *The Passion Translation*, *The Message*, *The Expanded Bible*, and *The Living Bible* often helped me to clarify meaning even when I did not end up using their exact words.

I did not use any word or phrase without finding justification for it in an existing translation, old or new.

TRANSLATIONS I CONSULTED

❖ *The Holy Bible*, King James Version. Oxford: Oxford University Press, c 1980.

❖ *The Holy Bible*, Revised Standard Version. New York: Thomas Nelson & Sons, 1953.

❖ Alter, Robert. *Strong as Death is Love, The Song of Songs: Ruth, Esther, Jonah, Daniel*. New York: W. W. Norton, 2015, pp 41–53.

❖ Bloch, Chana and Ariel Bloch. *The Song of Songs: A New Translation*. Berkeley: University of California Press, 1995.

❖ Pope, Marvin H. *Song of Songs: A New Translation with Introduction and Commentary*. New York: Doubleday, 1977.

❖ *The Complete Parallel Bible*. Oxford: Oxford University Press, 1994.

❖ Alter, Robert. *The Art of Bible Translation*. Princeton: Princeton University Press, 2019.

❖ Campbell, Gordon. *Bible: The Story of the King James Version*. Oxford: Oxford University Press, 2010.

❖ de Hamel, Christopher. *Bibles: An Illustrated History from Papyrus to Print*. Oxford: Bodleian Library, 2011.

❖ Falk, Marcia. *The Song of Songs: Love Lyrics from the Bible*. Waltham, MA: Brandeis University Press [University Press of New England]. 2004. Illustrations by Barry Moser.

❖ Knuth, Donald. *3:16: Bible Texts Illuminated*. Madison, WI: A-R Editions, Inc, 1991.

❖ Lewis, C. S. "Modern Translations of the Bible," in Walter Hooper, editor, *God in the Dock: Essays on Theology and Ethics*. Grand Rapids, MI: Eerdmans, 1972.

❖ Trible, Phyllis. *God and the Rhetoric of Sexuality*. Philadelphia: Fortress Press, 1978.

❖ Trithemius, Johannes. "About Calligraphy." "In Praise of Scribes: In Laude Scriptorium," http://williamwolff.org/wp-content/uploads/2009/06/TrithemiusScribes.pdf.

❖ Verdon, Timothy. *The Ecumenism of Beauty*. Orleans, MA: Mount Tabor Books (Paraclete Press), 2017. Susan Kanaga quotation, page 31.

CREDITS

INTRODUCTION

PAGE 9

Figure a. *Hebrew manuscript,* Hebrew scribe ©Norman Lebrecht/Bridgeman images.

Figure b. *Roman carving,* fragment of an inscription from a watchtower of the Collegium of vicus Beda, copy of a Roman original c 330. Ralph Rainer Steffens/Bildarchiv Steffens/Bridgeman Images.

Figure c. *Medieval manuscript,* Monk copying a manuscript from "The History of Rome" by Livy. By the Master of the Boqueteaux, c.1365. Ms 777, Bibliotheque Sainte-Genevieve, Paris, France. ©Archives Charmet/Bridgeman Images.

Figure d. *Arabic carving,* calligraphy on the wall of Eyup Mosque in Istanbul. Olena Rublenko/Shutterstock.com

PAGE 10:

Figure e. *Gutenberg Bible,* circa 1455. Bridwell Library Special Collections, Perkins School of Theology, Southern Methodist University.

PAGE 11:

Figure f. *King James Bible, 1611* edition. Author's collection.

Figure g. *Owen Jones,* illustrated page. University of Reading, Special Collections.

Figure h. *William Blake* print, *"To Tirzah."* The Morgan Library & Museum, New York. PML 954.

PAGE 12:

Figure i. *Laudes Beatae Mariae Virginis.* Special Collections and University Archives, University of Maryland Libraries.

Figure j. *Edward Johnston, Genesis page from Doves Press Bible.* Bridwell Library Special Collections, Perkins School of Theology, Southern Methodist University.

SONG OF SONGS IN CALLIGRAPHY
WITH COMMENTARY BY THE ARTIST

PAGE 58:

III: 6-11.   *"Pear, So Sweet."* Sumi-e (Japanese Brushstroke) and Shodo (Japanese Calligraphy) By artist Roslyn Levin. Used with permission.

PAGE 62:

IV: 8-9.   *"Layers of the Alps."* Photography by Simon Migaj. Used with permission.

PAGE 70:

V: 1.   *Portrait of a Bride,* Joseph James Jebusa Shannon. Private Collection Photo ©The Fine Art Society, London, UK. Bridgeman Images.

PAGE 72:

V: 2-6.   *Medieval cosmos, "The Flammarion Woodcut."* Bridgeman Images.
Deep Space Vortex. iStock photograph.

PAGE 80:

VI: 4-7.   *Small Versal U* from a Book of Hours. *Large Versal U* from an Antiphonal. Both letters, circa 1470, author's collection.

VI: 4-7.   *Presentation page* from Revised Standard Version Bible, Thomas Nelson & Sons, 1953. Author's collection.

PAGE 94:

VIII: 1-3.   *Opal ring.* Photography by Steve Dunwell.

PAGE 100:

VIII: 6-7.   *Roman letters* on Boston Public Library facade. Photography by Steve Dunwell.

PAGE 106:

VIII: 11-13. *Book of Hours.* The Morgan Library & Museum, New York. MS M.399.

ACKNOWLEDGMENTS

With Thanks

In addition to those who granted permission to use their illustrations, I owe thanks to many people who gave me help and encouragement to transform this scripture into calligraphy. I am grateful to my family and friends: Marilyn Brandt, the members of the venerable Saturday Morning Club, Dale Linder, Carol Christmas, Anne Bromer, David Friend, and Zoë Friend, as well as Ron Afzal, Cristle Collins Judd, Andrew Sowers, Phylis Tribble, Don Knuth, Barry Moser, and Stephen Kendrick. They made my ideas better by listening and looking. Debby Paddock, Cat Schaad, Steve Dunwell, and Colleen Mohyde looked after many details that got beyond me. The book itself took shape thanks to the fine team at Paraclete Press.